John –
Don't Settle for Less!
Chris Meyer

settle for

change your
negotiation
mindset and
change your
outcomes

CHRIS MEYER

Fedd Books
P.O. Box 341973
Austin, TX 78734

www.thefeddagency.com

Published in association with The Fedd Agency, Inc., a literary agency.

Cover Design: Christian Rafetto (www.humblebooksmedia.com)

ISBN: 9781957616858

LCCN: 2024910039

Printed in the United States of America

For Stacey.

I want to change your mind. Most negotiation books endeavor to walk you through some research and provide tactics to change your interactions and processes and thereby impact outcomes. This book stands apart by centering on the motives individuals bring into interactions and examining how these motives shape the interactions, processes, and outcomes.

The appropriate research will be included. The focus is also going to be a comparative of the current state of business literature with a Christian outlook. This is not a book of "Christian" negotiation tactics. This is not a book that will teach you how to be a better Christian negotiator. The book is going to compare current thought in negotiation to current thought in what is essentially Christian ethics—with the hope that this comparison will answer the question, "How can a Christian successfully negotiate in a secular world without being exploited?"

This is not a book written to convert you. This is not an exegesis or an apologetic interpretation. This is a negotiation book. I will focus on negotiation practices, but specifically on the motives that drive successful behaviors and how those behaviors impact relationships. I am a Christian, so that means I look at these ideas through the lens of my Christian faith.

This book comes out of a desire to change the way you think. I teach negotiation at the executive level, the MBA level, and the undergraduate level. Everyone, regardless of level and background, is concerned with getting the outcome they want. The anecdotal evidence says to protect your interests, to be cagey and reserved, and to hold your ground. There are some outdated negotiation strategies, programs, and trainings that espouse this view as well. I am going to present an argument that challenges that line of thinking and endeavor to move you toward understanding your interests, motives, openness with information, and relationships.

There is a better way to negotiate in your everyday life. There is a better approach than just moralizing. I support my position with research, logic, and ethical Christian thinking. I also apply the most current research. That said, this isn't a textbook. This book looks at the intersection of research and reality.

In this book I start with shared understanding. This is an unapologetically Christian look at our interactions, both personal and business related. I believe there are several reasons to treat people in a positive way. There are moral and ethical reasons, there are social justice reasons, there are business reasons, and there are religious reasons. I build a case for each of these viewpoints over the course of the book.

Part of this process includes the idea of choice. There is always a choice when it comes to our motives and behaviors.

> *"What a person plants, he will harvest. The person who plants selfishness, ignoring the needs of others—ignoring God!—harvests a crop of weeds. All he'll have to show for his life is weeds! But the one who plants in response to God, letting God's Spirit do the growth work in him, harvests a crop of real life, eternal life. So, let's not allow ourselves to get fatigued doing good. At the right time, we will harvest a good crop if we don't give up or quit. Right now, therefore, every time we get the chance, let us work for the benefit of all, starting with the people closest to us in the community of faith"* (Galatians 6:7-10, The Message).

Through this letter to the Galatian Christians, Paul tells us that we have a choice about how we live our lives—we can live to please ourselves or we can live to please God. Those are the only two choices. This has proven difficult for some in the business world. I've been asked many times how a Christian should negotiate. *It can't be the same two choices? Surely, we have the opportunity to be tough negotiators? The business world demands this.*

Most everyone is looking for a world that is safe, fair, and manageable. The world that we live in is not like that. Our everyday life is filled with uncertainty. It is evident in our personal lives when we make comments like, "It is what it is" or "Life's not fair" in response to someone's pain. It's evident in our business life when we use rhetoric to describe the process in which we are caught up, such as, "We need this win" or "We have to get whole on this deal." In our efforts to live in a world that is safe, fair, and manageable, we create a world that is protective, self-serving, and biased in our interactions with others.

This leads us to strive to take the fear of uncertainty out of our everyday lives, which leads to substandard outcomes and substandard lives.

Part of understanding and getting better in our interactions is understanding our identity in the world. Who are we? How do people view us? Are these two selves the same, or are they different? Are they the same to you, that is, do you think that you are presenting a consistent identity to the world as how you see yourself?

Oswald Chambers, in his book *Baffled to Fight Better*, tells us that it's not what a disciple does that makes them a disciple, but rather it's being "good in His motives" that makes a disciple. As a Christian, when you hear this, *you probably think, well, of course, the motive is very important, but when it's put into practice, it doesn't seem to work as easily as this.* We live in a dangerous world, and that danger elicits fear. That fear impacts our motive, and we try to control our interactions with others. Our motive becomes protective, self-serving, and biased. We try to reduce the uncertainty of the interaction. All of this works together to constrain our interactions and our outcomes.

I wrote this book out of a perceived gap between secular negotiation and Christian negotiation. I worked as a business professional who focused on negotiation for nine years. I worked in small businesses, where the very life of the company was dependent on my negotiations. I have first-hand experience with the reality of negotiation, with real consequences. I revisit some of these experiences throughout the book. But this isn't a book about my own anecdotal experiences with negotiation. After nine years in small businesses and high-tech start-ups, I went back to school to study and get my PhD in organizational behavior. Going back as an experienced student allowed me to have some perspective on the types of business problems that fascinated me. I gravitated toward studying organizational fairness, motivation, team dynamics, and, finally, negotiation. I would cluster all these topics under the heading of human interaction. When we break it down, negotiation is a human interaction that includes aspects from motivation, team dynamics, social psychology, and decision-making. In this book, I include my firsthand experience with the research behind negotiation.

While I was in the business world, I worked in sales—essentially, I was a negotiation professional. I was trained by other professional negotiators. I learned about things like presenting the return on investment, selling the benefits, and closing the deal. I learned about some of the softer skills, like building the relationship, networking (a brutal reality for an introvert like me), and even emotional intelligence. I then went to a secular, public university to study for my PhD. I spent four years dedicated to the research behind the human interactions that fascinated me so much while in the business world. I studied organizational fairness, motivation, and teams in detail. I studied and taught the broad topic of organizational behavior—why people do the things they do in organizations. And I studied and taught negotiation.

After graduate school, I took a job at a private Christian university. I thought I would feel free. I thought I would be beyond the duress that I felt in both my business and secular university life. In both of those organizational experiences, I felt that, while I was Christian, I had to leave part of that behind when I went to work or school. The research didn't segregate Christian organizational behavior and regular organizational behavior. Most of the people who I worked with were ambivalent toward Christianity at best, and some were even hostile.

It made me think that maybe there was a gap between the Christian business world and the secular business world. That we were forced to bridge or ignore faith while we were at work. I had a hard time explaining how people who were successful in business and called themselves Christian could act no differently than non-Christian businesspeople, especially when it came to negotiation. Why did people think that cutthroat tactics were ok to further the business and their career on Monday but on Sunday embrace "Love thy neighbor"? The gap was real.

Because of my job teaching at a Christian university, early in my academic career I was asked repeatedly, "How should I negotiate... as a Christian?" It's a strange question to me. I came from a completely secular background in my negotiation training, as most (all) negotiation training is secular, in that it has no component or focus on the impact religion or spirituality may have on the interaction.

This question of who you are and how you are perceived by your peers and colleagues is likely one that is important. It may have even plagued you at some point. This book is essentially about your identity and reconciling it within the workplace. As Christians, we often find ourselves in the position of justifying behaviors at work. We say things like, "Well, it's only business," or "That's how it works in the business world" to make room for poor behavior. We look at news stories about embezzlers, tax cheats, inside traders, and liars, and we say, *Thank God I'm not like that.* But daily, when we interact with people, we use half-truths and even lies. We manipulate to ensure our own gain at the expense of others; it's called parasitic value creation. Rather than being open and building others up, we guard our own outcomes.

I raise the question again. How should a Christian businessperson negotiate? Is there a different method of negotiation for the secular versus the Christian—a different way to conduct business? If you aren't a cutthroat business person, will you end up getting less? The answer is no.

While people aren't born negotiators, it's not luck or personality. Negotiation is a skill. There is a way to be a good business negotiator, and maintain your Christian ethics. It takes deliberate thought and practice.

How can Christians reconcile collaborative versus competitive styles in negotiation? How does a Christian be as gentle as a lamb and also "subdue the earth?" This book is an attempt to answer some of the questions that have plagued Christians and business people since Jesus Christ told the rich young ruler to sell everything he owned, give it to the poor, and follow Him. Since those days, and probably before, the question has been: how can I balance a faithful life with a profitable and successful life?

Negotiation is a difficult human interaction. It is filled with ambiguity. The world has taught us through anecdotes and myths. We have been given rhetoric like "kill or be killed." But the words of God are clear on the idea of motive. There's not a lot of ambiguity about the focus of our life. Why should we pause this ideal in the business world?

> *For what does it profit a man to gain the whole world and lose his soul? (Mark 8:36)*

> *For what will it profit a man if he gains the whole world and forfeits his soul? Or what shall a man give in return for his soul? (Matthew 16:26)*

I don't think Jesus is repeating himself, but he obviously said it with enough conviction that at least two of the disciples wrote it down. The business world is built around the idea of profit. Profit is not bad. In fact, I think Jesus Christ is advocating for profit in these passages. This instance, recorded by both Matthew and Mark, asks the question about profit in a very interesting way.

Jesus doesn't say, take up your cross and follow me because profit is the wrong path to follow. Jesus says that there is no profit in losing your soul.

Jesus tells us not to follow profit to the extent that we disregard long-term—here, He is talking about eternal—profit. He doesn't say, don't gain the whole world; he says, don't gain the whole world at the expense of your soul. He's telling us that we don't understand profit. Ever the teacher, Jesus is saying, "Yes, your goal is profit, and by the way, don't be mistaken in what is meant by profit. Get your profit, but make sure your motive is right. Make sure you don't forfeit your identity."

Jesus is not in it for short-term gain; he's playing the long game. If he were in it for short-term gain, he would have conceded to Satan when he was tempted in the wilderness. Why not turn the stones into bread? If Jesus thinks like you and me, "What's in it for me? How do I meet my goals? How do I get my outcome?" then, of course, he would take that short-term gain. He was hungry! The immediate gain—the one that we often focus on in our business dealings—was to satisfy His own needs, now! But with a long-term vision, Christ never forfeits His soul, or my soul, or your soul. Rather, he is motivated by joint gain. He wants the best outcome for you, me, and Himself. We'll take a much deeper look at this idea of joint gain throughout the book.

This book is my attempt to apply long-term vision while focusing on joint gain from a Christian perspective to the business and personal negotiations of today. I apply Christian principles to the most recent research and thought on negotiation. Many business leaders struggle with negotiation and multitudes of books have been written on the subject. This book applies consistent ideas and strategies from secular research with a Christian worldview.

When we apply the principles that God gives us to the strategies from the scientific literature, it should provide outcomes that are more positive on a number of different fronts. It's easy to look at the short-term outcome and quantify it in most negotiations. I also want to focus on the gain for the other involved parties. I want to focus on the long-term benefits of reputation, trust, and relationships. And I want to focus on Godly outcomes.

"And those who belong to Christ Jesus have crucified the flesh with its passions and desires. If we live by the Spirit, let us also keep in step with the spirit. Let us not become conceited, provoking one another, envying one another" (Galatians 5:24-26).

Paul was talking to the early church in this passage, but he was also talking directly to the businesspeople of today. You need to crucify the selfish desires of your flesh to keep in step with the Spirit of God. You need to be a positive force in the business community, not provoking or envying. This is difficult for most. It doesn't mean we are to have no desire or aspiration. It's an invitation to have the right focus for our desire and aspiration.

"On behalf of this man I will boast, but on my own behalf I will not boast, except of my weaknesses—though if I should wish to boast, I would not be a fool, for I would be speaking the truth; but I refrain from it, so that no one may think more of me than he sees in me or hears from me. So, to keep me from becoming conceited because of the surpassing greatness of the revelations, a thorn was given me in the flesh, a messenger of Satan to harass me, to keep me from becoming conceited. Three times I pleaded with the Lord about this, that it should leave me. But he said to me, 'My grace is sufficient for you, for my power is made perfect in weakness.' Therefore, I will boast all the more gladly of my weaknesses, so that the power of Christ may rest upon me. For the sake of Christ, then, I am content with weaknesses, insults, hardships, persecutions, and calamities. For when I am weak, then I am strong" (2 Corinthians 12:5-10).

The Apostle Paul had many reasons to boast. He was a Roman citizen and a leader in the Jewish community as a Pharisee. He was moving up the "corporate" ladder. He started out holding the coats while Stephen was stoned and moved up to running his own persecutions. He was being noticed. He was an important figure in both Jewish and Roman circles.

We all long to be noticed, some more than others. We all strive to move up the corporate ladder. We all look for ways to be more, get more, and even give more. There are countless books, training courses, gurus, ideas, and research that point the way for us to be successful in business. And many of us reading this are successful. And many are still trying to be more successful.

But we all have our thorns.

Are you content with weakness? Do you want to negotiate or work with people who insult you? Persecute you? We live in an imperfect and broken world. We try to do business in a manner that glorifies God, or at the very least, doesn't horrify God.

I return to the passages, written by Paul, who describes himself as everything from set apart for the Gospel (Rom 1:1) to chief among sinners (1 Tim 1:15). Then, In 2 Corinthians 12:9-11, Paul recognizes his weakness and God's grace. But more, He BOASTS of his weakness. "When I am weak, I am strong," he writes and then goes on to list his weaknesses—insults, hardships, persecutions, and calamities—as his strengths.

Paul sees how God uses his frailties to show His glory. This is not what we generally do in the business world. We don't list our failures and weaknesses, especially when we are up against tough negotiators. But, if we think about our motive in the negotiation—a motive of Joint Gain—weakness is insignificant. If the focus is on Joint Gain, the gain of all parties involved in the negotiation, what becomes more important is how we work together in the interaction.

It is my sincere hope that you will read this book and learn how to be a better negotiator. More than that, it is my hope that you read this book, see the principles at work in human behavior, and use your interactions in life to show the glory of God. It is my hope that I can show you that it is possible to do well in your daily negotiations and not have to compromise Christian principles. You can do well in your business life, in your life in general, and do it in a God-pleasing manner.

Let me help you with this particular thorn.

reconfiguring
what we think
about
NEGOTIATING

Much of our life happens in a competitive, win-focused environment. Most of the time it's easy to see the competitive ideal at our workplace. We have quotas, throughput, waste, and other less obvious ways that we know whether we are winning. At home, we check kids' report cards, develop chore charts, and ask who cooked dinner last or cleaned the garage. Our recreation is focused on winning football games, board games, or backyard games. We wear watches that track how many steps we take and compare those outcomes with our friends' totals. We have developed a culture that actively promotes the winners—winners get parades. Professor Edgar Schein from MIT says that most people believe if you aren't winning, you are losing. Take a minute to really, deeply consider that statement. If you are not actively winning, you are losing.

There are a lot of aspects of life that are competitive in nature. I'm not here to tell you not to compete. I'm going to try to convince you that there's a better way to compete when it comes to negotiation in both your business and personal life. I want you to think critically about your interactions and to be open to thinking about these interactions in a different way.

Let's define what I mean by "win." When we think about a win in the context of a sporting event, we are talking about scoring more than the others involved in the contest. It can be one more touchdown, one more basket, eating one more hotdog, ending up with all the chips at the end of the poker game—we have so many ways to keep score.

We invent ways to keep score. We invent contests that demand a score. We embed contests within our contests—you can shoot three-point shots during halftime of an NBA game to win prizes. But it's not just sports. We keep score in our

chapter 1

WINNING

businesses. We know who the top salesperson is in the company. We know who the employee of the month is. We have annual reviews that score our progress. We are rank ordered.

At home, we can check the score in our bank accounts from an app on our phone. We know who took the trash out last. We know who cooks. We know who cleans. We know if the kids keep their room clean. We know who has homework done, and we know the grades. The teachers update my kids' grades daily, and I can check them daily. I don't. If I want to know, I ask my wife. She knows their score every day.

We happily tell everyone around us who is winning and, by default, who is losing.

I want to be clear that I am not against winning, except when it comes to negotiation. We all have some level of competitive spirit within us, and games are designed to appeal to that nature. But when it comes to our interactions with others, we should think twice about the desire to win as our outcome.

To win is to acquire victory. To win is to defeat, subdue, dominate. You may be thinking that's exactly what you want to do in your business life. You may even be thinking that's what you want to do in your personal life. You (most likely) would say that to win with integrity is your goal. That's the hallmark of a good negotiator: winning with integrity. But there is more to it than just winning with integrity. When you win—even with integrity— there is a loser.

There is a loser.

This culture of score keeping has some benefits. Had my parents been able to check my grades daily they may have given me some positive course corrections. Without annual reviews, employees would be lacking the critical feedback that is necessary to move them in the right direction. Sports are entertaining, and I'm not suggesting we play for the fun of the game. I like scores and winning as much as everyone else. I'm not suggesting that all winning is bad.

I am suggesting that a win motive in your negotiations is a short-sighted strategy. I'm suggesting that you can do better than that. What about win-win as a strategy, you might wonder? Fair question.

I suggest the win-win strategy is just a disguised way to look for a win. In the win-win outlook on negotiation, there is still a first winner. Everyone else is a loser, even if we call it a win.

Most people negotiate out of convenience, not a consistent, deliberate strategy. They take what can be taken from an interaction, hope it comes close to a goal, and move on to the next interaction. There is a pervasive view of negotiation as a competition with winners and losers. If we aren't entering a negotiation with a clear view of our motives, interests, and biases, we don't have the appropriate information to negotiate.

And there is a strong desire to win negotiations.

Almost every semester, I teach a class on negotiation. I read a lot of papers about negotiation written by students who are successful business people returning to school to earn an MBA. These papers consistently contain rhetoric about the desire to "win, dominate, achieve, defeat, triumph, prevail" and other terms that make it clear that business people are keeping score in their negotiations.

I do think you should keep score in your negotiations, but not in the way that is typically done. Most score the wrong thing.

The way we often decide if we won a negotiation doesn't make sense. It's like the punter claiming he won because he kicked more times and for more distance than the punter on the other team. It's a way to keep score, but it's not really what we're trying to measure.

My background before my graduate work was in sales. There were a lot of sales training classes that focused on selling benefits to customers. There were a lot of mentors, directors, and managers who told me about how solution selling helps people to positively impact their business. I was taught about score keeping. The salesperson has a quota and is trying to meet the quota or exceed the quota to make more money, get a good review, or win the sales competition. Winning was the culture, the whole point, even if it didn't lead to long-term success.

Motive

Ask people who are deliberate about how they negotiate what's the best way to negotiate. People will quickly reply with the popular answer: win-win. It sounds good, but let's take a deeper look at what it really means.

Think of the rhetoric behind this short and very catchy phrase. What are we really saying if we say win-win? What do we think of when we use that phrase? Most people think WIN. And when I activate that thought, I am actually thinking about my win, not yours. Business is competitive. Life is competitive. We live in a culture of striving.

What if we change the rhetoric? Is winning the negotiation a proper motive? When you want to win, is it really the win that drives you?

If you are trying to win in an interaction in your organization, what does it represent? What's behind that organizational win? Do you want the negotiation to go your way so that you gain respect? Do you want to demonstrate some expert knowledge? Do you want to leverage that win into a better position and, with that, an increased quality of life? Or are you thinking about an interaction that's more personal. Maybe you are trying to gauge the respect your husband will give your opinion or whether your kids will share a critical value.

When we talk about a win-focused negotiator or an outcome that demonstrates a win, we're often talking about achieving a specific position in the negotiation. A position is a singular outcome formed by our limited knowledge and the biases that we carry with us into the negotiation. Positions are easily quantifiable; they are the dollars and cents, the tangible aspects of a negotiation. Winning is achieving those positions without giving up much from those positions in the process.

Whether this is a business or a personal negotiation, there is a drive to win. Noted management scholar Edgar Schein maintains that business professionals, and people in general, work from a basis of competition. And he's not alone in his position that people view interactions as zero-sum. There are a number of studies that claim individuals either enter a negotiation with a competitive perspective, or a motive to win, or they adopt one within the first few minutes of the interaction.

That's a powerful statement.

People view their interactions as zero-sum interactions. That means I think everything that you gain is a loss to me. It means I think you can't get a benefit unless I take a loss. It means every dollar you gain comes directly from my pocket.

We want to win because we don't want to lose. It's a lack mindset. And highly unproductive.

I was giving a presentation recently, and a member of the audience was the CEO of a large organization. He was very attentive as I led a discussion about winning versus losing in a negotiation. I presented a case study example of a not-for-profit organization negotiating with a large donor. Several items were of great value to the donor organization but had no value and no cost to the not-for-profit organization.

We talked in the room about the ease with which the not-for-profit could give these simple concessions to the donor. There had been bad blood in the past between the two organizations and this could go a long way to heal the rift. We talked about how appreciative the donor organization would be and how far this would go toward a positive relationship. The donor, who had felt slighted in the past, could have a tangible demonstration of their importance to the not-for-profit organization. The not-for-profit could make a tangible demonstration of their care for the community and their donors.

All it would take is conveying a benefit at no cost without demanding or expecting something in return.

It was a great idea.

The room agreed.

The not-for-profit should give these benefits to the donor. All bad blood would be healed. The organizations would have a bright future together.

Then the discussion started. Well, what if we gave the donor organization some of these benefits? Not all of the benefits. Why would we give them all? We should definitely benefit the donor organization, maybe we could give them fifty percent of the issues that are important to them? That seems good, fifty percent or forty percent. We should definitely benefit them.

Maybe thirty percent. Competitive arousal at work.

Competitive arousal is the idea that when faced with a situation that increases pursuit of a victory, individuals can become so competitive that they become ferocious combatants fighting desperately to achieve their win. Competitive arousal has been linked to a number of dramatically bad decisions in the business world. It causes individuals to abandon rationality in the desire to achieve a win at all costs.

Then the CEO chimed in and led a discussion. The decision was to give them a slight benefit, but not too much. Hold some of the benefit in reserve. Keep some of that benefit "in our pocket" so that we don't give it all to them.

Remember, the benefit had no value to the not-for-profit. The benefit had no cost to the not-for-profit. The benefit had no longevity; that is, if it were kept and not distributed, it would disappear. If it wasn't offered to and used by the donor, it was gone. Wasted.

And a room full of intelligent people decided to waste that benefit, rather than give it to another party. This happened immediately after my presentation, which was focused on the desirability of benefiting others in a negotiation. I presented a number of studies that showed the positive outcomes of benefiting others in a negotiation. I presented the research about building the relationship. I presented the research about the benefits of collaborative negotiation.

I was both shocked and not shocked at the same time.

I asked the CEO, who had vacated his seat and moved to the front of the room, "Why?"

Why did he and the rest of the room decide to hold back a benefit that had great meaning for the donor organization and no meaning at all for the organization he was representing in the case study? His answer is indicative of what happens in business negotiations every day.

He said, "We wanted to win."

But there is no change in your outcome either way?

"We can't win if they get more."

Competitive arousal at work.

This is something that is consistent in the research. It's also consistent in the anecdotal evidence. People want to win. This was a case study about a not-for-profit charity business and a major donor. Imagine how much these individuals would want to win if the case was about a for-profit business and a supplier. Now imagine how this plays out when there is real money involved. This contributes to the competitive nature of business and society today.

So, how can you use this information in your day-to-day negotiations?

If everyone is competing and trying to win, so what? Shouldn't you try to win, too?

When faced with negotiations against parties that are trying to win, why would you want to do anything but win yourself? And to win, that means the others involved aren't going to win. And the people who don't win are... it's ok, you can say it.

Losers.

You don't want to be a loser, so, by definition, you have to win. That's how people justify the motive that drives their day-to-day negotiations. Think back to the CEO and the not-for-profit case study. Winning drove a room full of people to deny a benefit to another party in the interaction just to preserve the perception of their win.

We love the win-win idea because we genuinely want the other party to benefit from the interaction. At the same time, we want to win.

My former student, Kenneth, a professional salesperson, calls his version of this story "stupid sales." Working under the assumption that the other party is looking for a win but is also unconcerned about Kenneth's win, I think it's a pretty good assumption. Most of the interactions that I have are with people who want to know how to win at negotiation. The research tells us that even if people enter a negotiation with a cooperative or collaborative mindset, within fifteen minutes, they drop back into a competitive negotiation style. That makes it safe to assume that you will be negotiating with a competitive negotiator.

This competitive nature is pretty common. There's a lot of anecdotal evidence to support it. There are also countless books that focus on leverage, power, getting an advantage, etc. This library of competitive tactics is useful in that you can easily understand the competitive negotiator.

The competitive negotiator will talk about wins or winning. Their focus during preparation and planning is on advantage or power. The competitive negotiator doesn't share information, makes demands, threatens to walk away, and talks a lot about the alternatives that he or she could easily take. They are focused on position and unwilling to move far from it. If you are a collaborative negotiator who brings value to the interaction, you can persuade very easily.

Negotiating with a competitive negotiator is easy. They are focused on winning. So, give them a win.

Everyone who takes the time and effort to negotiate wants to get ahead. They want to achieve more through the interaction than they could achieve on their own.

In the context of winning, even if the negotiation is beneficial to both parties, the problem arises when a negotiator sees someone other than themself as winning.

Sit with that idea for just a minute.

I know what you're thinking—*everyone does that except me. I'm happy to see other people win.*

One study concludes that when a person receives an offer from another party, they should always counter that offer, even if it is exactly what they were trying to achieve. If they don't counter, they will seem too eager to accept, and the other party will feel like the offer was too generous. They call it the winners' curse.

The person "won" the negotiation by having his first offer accepted. Yet, oddly, because there was no counter, the perception of who "won" shifts. Suddenly, the person who made the first accepted offer is unhappy with the deal. Even though they researched and felt good with their offer, now they feel like they left money on the table.

The accepted offer was an acceptable outcome for both parties, yet now one side feels as though it lost.

Why? Because their focus was on winning.

Having an offer accepted, in this case, was meaningless.

Achieving a positive outcome was worthless.

Winning was the only thing that mattered.

Competitive arousal.

Keith Murnighan told a story of offering money to MBA students in class as part of a research study. Students were put into pairs and one student in each pair was to decide about the distribution of money. The student was given a choice of keeping ten dollars for herself and providing eight dollars to her partner; or, she could keep twelve dollars for herself, and the other student would get twenty.

There was no pooling or splitting allowed. In this low-stakes experiment the students typically chose to take less money (ten dollars) so that they would have more than their counterparts (who received eight dollars). This is a win-win outcome. There are eighteen dollars of value. Eighteen dollars that the students didn't have before this exercise. Thirty-two dollars was available—but in order to win, most chose to take less for themselves and in the process, provide even less to the others involved.

Essentially they are saying, I like win-win as long as I win more than the others involved.

You may find it hard to believe, but the research is sound.

Max Bazerman and some colleagues recreated the research and found that parties that shared some affiliation were willing to benefit other parties more, even if they didn't get the same benefit. But those parties that were outside of the group, those that were not affiliated, would choose the "win" over the others, even if it meant they received less themselves in the overall outcome.

Competitive arousal at work again.

That brings us back to "stupid sales." While allowing the other party to win is not necessarily a bad idea, I think the biggest issue with negotiators trying to win is the motive.

When we take on a motive to win, we are ultimately trying to achieve safety in our daily lives. We want the world to be safe, so we take control over our positions. Our motive is to remove some of the ambiguity in the interaction, and by winning, we know what our outcome will be. At the very worst, we know the position that we are hanging on to, even at the cost of the other parties' gain and the relationship.

Attitude

I think sometimes we downplay the power of attitude, not just in our negotiations but also in our daily lives. The motive we carry into the negotiation impacts our attitude in the negotiation.

So, how important is our attitude? What does the persistent affective and cognitive state of the individuals involved in an interaction matter to the outcome? You're probably thinking, *this is an easy question,* but is it?

We think about attitude in a limited way. Most view attitude as a vaguely positive or negative approach to an issue or problem. We say she has a good attitude, or he has a bad attitude about an issue or a situation. Sometimes, we ascribe the impact of attitude to a relationship; he has a bad attitude toward his boss.

But attitude goes much deeper. Attitude is pervasive and persistent. And it isn't just good or bad. Attitude can be about how you approach the interactions that you face each day. Do you think the best of people? Do you try to lift people up? Are you willing to benefit your business partners, even if it seems that they might be doing better than you? Are you a jealous person? Are you willing to share information? Are you open to new ideas?

We want the world to be fair. It isn't.

This is a struggle for many people; it's a struggle for me. The research calls it equity sensitivity. How important is it to you that your outcomes match or exceed your perceived inputs? Everyone likes to think that they bring something important to the table, and everyone likes to think they will get a return on that important offering.

That's a pretty persistent attitude in the world. There are not a lot of people or organizations that stand up for unfairness in the world. So, if everyone has an attitude that supports fairness, why do we have issues with it? The problem with an attitude toward fairness is that we tend to overestimate the value that we bring to the interaction while simultaneously undervaluing what others bring. This can tend to have a pretty detrimental effect on the whole fairness equation. If you have an attitude of equity sensitivity, and it's pretty common in our culture, but you overvalue your own contributions and undervalue others', you're going to see a lot of unfairness in the world.

The attitude toward winning is another part of this difficulty. Remember the story about MBA students and their desire to reach a win-win solution as long as they won more? Or the CEO who wants to hold back some benefit just to be sure the outcome isn't unfair? This is the win attitude. It creeps into our rhetoric, and from there, it rents space in our heads.

Think about the words you say when you are getting ready to negotiate. How do you talk about the process? How do you talk about the other parties? Do you use words like "fight," "win," "against," and "opponent"? All of these are terms that indicate that there is a contentious win-lose attitude at hand. And this attitude drives your behavior in the interaction.

Behavior

We want the world to be safe, fair, and manageable. Our behavior is the manifestation of our attempts to manage the world. Everyone experiences the world differently, we all make sense of our world based on our experience and personality. Differences between people are simultaneously the best and the worst parts of humanity. Without the diversity that our differences bring, we end up with lower outcomes, fewer innovations, and a world of less. Embracing those differences leads us down a path that demands understanding.

One of the drivers of our negotiations are the expectations that we take into the interaction. Think of the win-win perspective on negotiation. If our motive is to win, then our attitude is to put ourselves above others in the interaction, and our behavior will support those two fundamentals. If we need to tell a white lie to move the win in our direction, it's ok. If we need to hide some facts in the interaction, we do that to serve our outcome.

Competitive arousal is going to be an important aspect of our behavior as well. If we are pursuing that win at all costs, it allows for some pretty bad behavior to creep into our daily interactions. This is how we end up down a path of lying in a negotiation or hiding facts, misrepresenting our real position. These behaviors are bad for outcomes. The research tells us that lying in negotiation leads to lower outcomes. When we lie and misrepresent our positions the other parties involved rely on those lies and that leads them away from possible outcomes and benefits that may be available.

When we frame our negotiations with win-win rhetoric, it leads us to something very specific. We will obfuscate and obscure; we will be less quick to share information. We will also be unwilling to ask genuine questions about the best scenario or outcome for the other parties. Trusting the motives of others becomes difficult. And when trust breaks down, the negotiation suffers. (Think about a few of your interactions from the recent past and honestly assess what you did and why you did it.)

When we have a win focus, we think about the risk that it poses to share information. "If I tell my boss what I want during my annual review she will…" insert your fear here. So, we see our interactions as adversarial. If we have a win mentality, that assumes a loss for others involved in the negotiation. As much as we want to think there is a win-win outcome, one of the parties is going to get a bigger, better, faster, or stronger outcome. That makes them the winner. And if they win, I lose.

The behavior in a win-focused negotiation is contentious. It's combative. It is value destroying, not value creating.

The Origin of Human Competitive Nature

What is the origin of this competitive nature?

In the 1960s, a researcher named Robert Axelrod wrote what is still one of the most interesting books on the competitive nature of human interactions. Axelrod studied individuals involved in what is called a Prisoner's Dilemma interaction. This experiment is famous for birthing the tit-for-tat negotiation strategy.

Tit-for-tat says that I begin in a cooperative stance, but I return any behavior that is presented to me. This means if I am faced with a competitive negotiator, I should be competitive. If she withholds information, I should withhold information. If he lies, I should lie. If he cooperates, I should cooperate. But if the other party is being competitive, and I am returning that behavior, how would we ever get out of a contentious, competitive, win-driven cycle?

Why are we all so focused on this drive to win? Where does it come from?

I'm not sure we can completely explain the competitive nature of human beings. It's been around for as long as we've kept history.

The first recorded negotiation this world saw was a colossal failure. We don't know everything about the early days of this earth; we know what is reported by Moses many years after it happened in the book of Genesis. We know that God made a perfect world for humanity to inhabit. We know that there were two named individuals who lived in a garden in a community with the Almighty God. And we know that there was a competitive desire for more. Whatever you believe about the origin of the Earth, this story is instructive about the origin of the human competitive spirit.

The principal liar, the devil, arrived on the scene with some information and an offer. And it only worked because, as humans, we are driven to want more. We want more than we have, yes, but I'm talking about an even more insidious more.

The serpent came to Eve and said, "Hey, you've got it pretty good here." And Eve agreed. Then came the move that dirty negotiators still use today. "Yep, pretty good... but not great. You can't have this fruit. I mean, you could have this fruit, but you know, it's probably not the fruit for you. This fruit is only for God. He knows it will make you like Him..."

A dirty trick. Telling someone they can't have something (or pointing it out) only makes it more desirable. Ask any toddler. Tell them they can't have something, and it becomes the object they must have at all costs. And if you want to increase the effect, make it something that others possess. The serpent knew this.

"Do you want to be like God?" he asked Eve. Of course. This trick is still used today. It's why NBA players are spokesmen for signature lines of sneakers. Want to be like an All-Star NBA player? Want to shoot like Stephen Curry? Buy these shoes for $200. These are the shoes he wears. And they are hard to find, and that makes them even more desirable.

Don't think this isn't a negotiation.

Shoe manufacturers know it's a negotiation. They are using all the tricks to get you to provide them with a benefit. Like the serpent and Eve, you get a benefit, but not the benefit that is implied. The implication is that these shoes will make you into something that you are not; these shoes will impact your life in a way that you never thought possible. That's what makes it a competitive negotiation. If they used a collaborative negotiation, then we could work together with the sneaker manufacturers and benefit both parties more fully. The shoe manufacturers want your money, market share, and reputational effect, and the consumer wants something, too. Maybe the consumer wants style, performance, or that feeling of being included in something special.

Back to the garden. Let's focus on that negotiation for a minute. The serpent and Eve start to negotiate. The Serpent asks her, "Did God actually say not to eat this...?" You can almost hear the tone of voice. "Really?" Eve does what we all do in a negotiation, she embellishes her point, thinking that will make it stronger. "Right, he said don't even touch it—or you'll die." We do this, too. We tell our counterparts, "This is the most I can do/give. I can't go any higher." We say this because we think it makes our position stronger. What this does is lead us right into the trap. In reality, it makes us weaker.

Threats beget threats. It doesn't matter the context. It doesn't matter the prior trust, the starting point, or the relationship. Doubt me? Try it on your kids, your parents, or your spouse. "Take out the garbage, or else..." and see how it goes.

Look at the way the Almighty God negotiates in this instance. God started this interaction. He provided the initial value in the deal.

> *"The LORD God took the man and put him in the garden of Eden to work it and keep it. And the LORD God commanded the man, saying, 'You may surely eat of every tree of the garden, but of the tree of the knowledge of good and evil you shall not eat, for in the day that you eat of it you shall surely die'"* (Genesis 2:15-17).

He, who has everything, gave these people a perfect place to live, gave their lives purpose, and asked them to do one thing. Don't eat this specific fruit. Everything else is yours. Now, you may wonder why God had this specific restriction. I wonder that, too. Why is it that there is one specific fruit I can't eat? Only God knows.

Regardless, it's not an unrealistic restriction in organizational life. Bosses give us boundary conditions all the time. We sometimes know why we have a boundary condition, but not always. Sometimes, we know why our sales quota is what it is, why we have a specific revenue target, or why we have to cut waste as much as we do, but not always. There are times when it's just the way it is. Have you ever said, "...because I'm the parent, that's why..."?

It's frustrating to be in the position of having an undefined or ill-defined boundary condition. There is a well-known study in the field of organizational behavior titled, "On the folly of rewarding A while hoping for B" that looks at the mismatch between rewards and desires. This is one of the chief problems in negotiation as well. We reward behavior that doesn't really help us achieve the reason we are negotiating in the first place. More on that later.

Eve is faced with this dilemma. She walks into a negotiation, a competitive negotiation. She isn't prepared. The biggest issue with a competitive negotiation is the *all-or-nothing* thinking that it engenders. A competitive negotiation, by definition, assumes there are a fixed number of resources to be shared. Anything given up by one party benefits the other party. If I want to gain something in a competitive negotiation, I have to take it from someone else. Eve is deep in the competitive negotiation, and she's about to take something from Almighty God.

A chief problem in these competitive, zero-sum negotiations is the ambiguity of loss. What is it that I am losing to get to an agreement?

He is the Almighty God. He gave Adam and Eve everything. A perfect world was theirs. They were to take care of it, be fruitful and fill it, and not eat from one tree. But, as humans do, they wanted more. Not just more, they wanted everything. This is where we fail in negotiations. How do we look at having a perfect world and everything in it and get persuaded to eat the one fruit that was forbidden? Eve was persuaded. And then she persuaded Adam. Moses doesn't tell us how this went down, but I can imagine that Adam said something to the effect of, "Hey, give me a bite too. You don't get it all." He surely didn't want Eve to win and leave him behind as the loser.

Regardless of your beliefs about how the human race started, this is a powerful story. You can be a literalist and believe that Eve had a conversation with evil embodied in a serpent, or you can take it as a mythical story given as an illustration. Either way, this well-know story is part of the human story and represents the interactions that we have in our daily lives. Think of the rhetoric used in a negotiation. Usually, there is a good guy and a bad guy. We typically see ourselves as the good guys and the others, those with whom we are negotiating, as the bad guys. The snakes.

Because of our biases, we view our own actions as good and the actions of others as bad. Remember equity sensitivity? We think that we bring more value and others bring less.

How do we go into a negotiation, achieve the benefit that we are there to achieve, and demand more? What makes us so willing to take, demand, lie, cheat, and connive to get everything, with no concern for anyone else?

How do you want those in the business world to view you? Why do you think the euphemism exists that when someone is dishonest, we refer to them as snakes. A snake represents a liar and a cheat. A snake is the devil, the enemy.

And a snake is how we refer to businesspeople with whom we don't want to do business. We don't trust them. We refer to them as if they were the devil because they act like the devil, the prince of liars. A snake in the grass is a phrase that we use to refer to someone who is unethical, untrustworthy, or suspicious to us.

You can't trust a snake.

The snake follows the letter of the law and exploits it for his own benefit. The snake makes you think that it is on your side. This is the trick of the enemy, and it's the same trick used by competitive negotiators. They make you think that what you are doing is ok when, in fact, it is not. They bend the truth enough that it benefits them. They do whatever it takes to win.

Competitive arousal.

The devil tricks us into thinking that taking advantage of people is "only business." Why would we separate what we do in our daily business lives and our daily home life? It's like the separation of your life into the sacred and the profane. On Sunday, you hold the door for old ladies, you put money in the offering plate, and you pray for your enemies. On Monday, you take advantage of your customers who don't have complete information, you squeeze your suppliers until they are losing money, or you treat employees in a deplorable fashion.

All this under the guise of "It's only business."

This viewpoint is reinforced by training programs and anecdotal evidence. The lack of trust, the idea that others are going to take advantage of us, is a powerful force.

What pushes us into this *win-at-all-costs* competitive style of interaction? How does this connection between thinking and acting push us to think and act in a self-focused and individualistic way?

The desperate need for control drives us forward to the competitive side of the interaction. We come by this as a proxy for the holy desire that God placed in us at creation.

> *"And God blessed them. And God said to them, 'Be fruitful and multiply and fill the earth and* **subdue it, and have dominion over the fish of the sea and over the birds of the heavens and over every living thing that moves on the earth.**' *And God said, 'Behold, I have given you every plant yielding seed that is on the face of all the earth, and every tree with seed in its fruit. You shall have them for food'"* (Genesis 1:28–29). (Emphasis added)

We were given a command. We were told to have dominion. But we confuse this. We get it into our heads that the subduing we are to do is over our fellow man. *It's just business, after all.* But this is not what God has commanded. The command is to subdue the earth (by filling it with other humans), and the dominion that was given was over the animals. This gets dramatically confused.

We have developed training sessions, classes, on-the-job training, and more that push this desire to hold dominion over others. It's fear. We fear the loss of control. Fear is the entrance for the enemy in our business dealings. Why do we hold back from expressing ourselves and our interests in the interaction? Fear. Fear of being hurt. Fear of someone taking advantage of us. Fear of ambiguity.

Fear can rule us, take advantage of us, and be the weapon of the enemy. Think of the places in your life that are driven by fear. Fear causes you to wonder about your coworkers' motives. Fear breaks up marriages, drives families apart, and keeps parents up at night, worrying about their kids' choices.

And fear is what keeps us from being open with people about our interests in a business setting. When we sit down with a customer, supplier, subordinate, boss, peer, etc., we aren't open and honest about the things that we should be open to discussing. We hide, obfuscate, lie, and otherwise obscure the truth of our reality. And this is a perspective problem. We can't see that our reality may not be everyone's reality. We see the world through our biases. We see the interactions through our lens. We can't and we don't allow others to have a different lens. We assume that everyone sees things the way we do, and this leads to distrust. Because we aren't open and honest, we assume that everyone is also hiding something. It's a vicious cycle. *I can't share with you because you didn't share with me, and you didn't share with me because I can't share with you.*

But it's easy to break the cycle.

Bring value to the interaction.

If we bring value, others will bring value. In a negotiation, value creation is not a gift to be given but the creation or provision of the outcome that will be distributed in the negotiation.

This is where people get lost in the idea. You may feel confused or skeptical. Not about creating value, but about being the FIRST to create value. Leading the initiative to create value. That's where you may have some difficulty. And it comes back to fear. The fear is that you will create value and that the other parties involved in the negotiation will take advantage of you. Why do you have that fear? Isn't that fear a weakness manifesting itself? If you are the party that creates value or brings value to an interaction, that puts you in a very positive position.

Fear of being taken advantage of is what has caused many of our current management ideas. This fear has birthed Management by Objective: we fear that our employees take advantage of the system and get paid while not contributing. Thus, structures are developed to (micro) manage them. We take this route believing it's measurable and fair. But really, it's easy. We don't have to think or understand. We just give everyone a plan under the guise of fairness and equity.

But this removes the perspective of each person. It's dehumanizing. It makes the ideas, the views, the wishes, and the dreams of each employee irrelevant. Context matters, and each interaction is somewhat idiosyncratic. We must take the person or persons involved in the interaction into account.

Remember the management study about aligning rewards? How could you forget "On the folly of expecting A while rewarding B?" The same can be said of our interactions. I have three children that are very different. If I try to motivate them all the same way, I may get lucky, and one will be moved. If I use a chore chart, I have one son who will sit and read and ignore chores because he's not motivated that way.

The same can be said for most of our negotiation tactics. Because of fear, we often don't take the perspective of others; we don't think through the objectives, the interests, and the emotions involved. We are looking for fair, and that's not good enough, because fair is subjective. Don't believe me? Go find a four-year-old and ask them about fair.

Think about it—why are you so afraid that the others involved in the negotiation are going to be unfair to you? Why are you afraid that you're going to get cheated?

It may have to do with a past relationship. It may have to do with the ambiguity you face daily. Or it may be that you don't feel trustworthy yourself. You may think that you would take advantage of the other party if given the opportunity. Would you? Would you benefit yourself at someone else's expense? What if no one would find out?

The idea that no one else will know is powerful and one that we have difficulty reconciling. We may think we would never take advantage of someone else. Not us; we're righteous. But we often live in the fear that others, when faced with the opportunity to take advantage of someone, will take it. And that same fear often undermines our actions when we think no one is watching.

So, if we shouldn't run our business based on fear, how should we run it? This question is for everyone. No matter your position in your organization, you are running your own personal business. It has taken me some time in my career to realize this. The decisions that you make and the processes that you put in place to govern your daily work are the strategy of your own business. How you think about your daily interactions will impact what you do.

There is a link between your cognition and your behavior, that is, what you think impacts what you do. If you think that you can control or impact your outcomes in the organization with the work that you do, that will impact your behavior. Similarly, if you think that you have little or no control, you'll do what you can to take control.

You will try to win.

There is something strong at work in our culture. It's something small, insidious, barely noticeable. But it's there. There is an effort to rank everyone and everything. All the time.

Well, this is great, you may think. *When I want to buy something, I can easily go online, read reviews, and know what is good and what is not good. When it comes time to give out raises, I can rank people based on productivity, or some easy metric, and know who gets the big raise and who gets the reprimand. It makes things easy. If I can just look at which salesperson sold the most or which purchasing agent got the biggest discount rate or which professor published the most or had the most A students, then I can apportion the resources and rewards fairly.* And while there is a transactional truth in this evaluative idea, as relational beings, it's not the whole story.

When we score everything, we're subject to the scoring system. If we don't clearly think through aligning the scoring system with the overall objective, our system is flawed. For example, if you only look at the star rating of a product on Amazon, you won't take into account that a negative review can be connected to the fact a person ordered the wrong color, wrong size, wrong thing altogether, or maybe they don't know how to use the product. Stars don't tell the whole story.

Salespeople are often evaluated on numbers that may not be relevant to the goals of the organization. If my organization is small and is trying to be acquired by a larger organization, I likely need to build the market of those using my product/technology. If my small company is trying to get funding from banks or venture capital, I probably need to show some positive cash flow and profitability. In the first scenario my sales force can discount the product and move as much as possible at a price close to or even below cost. In the second scenario I need

to sell at a profit, and the higher the profit the better. The focus is, when my sales force negotiates a price with the customer, do my measures support the goals of both the salespeople and the organization? If I implement a system that rewards salespeople for quantity of sales, it doesn't support the second goal, but it may support the first goal.

A better scoring mechanism for the first goal would be to reward sales based on market penetration. Reward sales in the second scenario based on overall profitability. And, you must also think through the organizational culture, market, competition, specific individuals you are measuring, level of experience or skill, and on and on.

It's not easy.

But we try to make it easy. When we buy a car, we have a price or monthly payment in mind. If we walk out the door meeting those goals, we win. But we often don't feel like we win.

Every time we rank ourselves, our products, our competitors, we make sure that people know who the winner is, and by default, who is the loser.

As I've already noted, the win/lose paradigm works when there is a zero-sum situation, like a basketball game. Business is rarely zero-sum.

Consider the gamification of the world we live in. We track everything. We have social comparisons of the steps we take and the calories we eat. Video games happen in real time and against real opponents. We no longer try to get a high score or a personal best; instead, we try to beat everyone else so that we can dance in their faces and show our superiority.

You may be thinking, *Hey, there are winners and losers. Games are competitive, and we should celebrate winners.* I agree, if you are talking about games. But do you perform a celebration dance in your spouse's face if you get her to take out the garbage? Or if you get to choose the restaurant for date night? Winners and losers don't work in the context of relationships. And every negotiation involves human relationships.

We live in a world that has embraced gamification. We understand every interaction through meticulous tracking, scoring, and logging. Top salespeople get trips, prizes, or bonuses. Reducing delivery time or waste is tied to departmental outcomes. None of these are bad practices, except that they shift the focus away from the goals of the organization and onto the individual or small group. What would you do to make the last sale that puts you in the lead and could give you a huge personal benefit? Salespeople on the same team shouldn't be in competition. It puts people in the situation of working against a teammate.

This idea is insidious. We don't see how much it has infiltrated our lives, and we don't recognize the impact. Starbucks, McDonalds, and many other retailers understand the impact of gamification. Starbucks emails me "challenges" weekly. They tell me if I buy a certain selection of products I can win benefits. As much as I want to win Starbucks for Life, I can't bring myself to order every super sweet, whipped cream, fruit and nut coffee. I like coffee, often with steamed milk, but every time they email and tell me I didn't complete the challenge, they are letting me know I lost. And I think, "I never win these Starbucks challenges. Maybe I should just go somewhere else for coffee?"

It has an impact on our psyche and on organizational outcomes.

Some people get wrapped up in the winning and losing of gamification. Our susceptibility has to do with our upbringing, personality, and values. But the truth of the matter is that many today are so accustomed to the gamification of this world that it dominates unconscious thought. If you are a step counter, have you ever gotten off the couch at 10:30 p.m. to walk around the block three times to hit your goal? Have you walked partway on the third trip around, calculating where to turn, so that you hit that goal as you walk back into the house? I have. I bet I'm not the only one.

Gamification elevates the win-lose perspective and makes it more important than it really is. Yes, the examples that I am giving are extreme, but think about it in the context of your last team meeting, or the last department get-together, or your last client visit. If you celebrate the win in front of your client, what are the consequences? What about if the client celebrates in front of you?

Now, how does that change if you celebrate gains together? Interesting question. We'll get to that later.

Part of this gamification is enabled by the instant gratification culture in which we live. We live in an Instagram life. People post pictures to demonstrate where they fall in the social hierarchy. We all want to win that game.

What if we weren't focused on winning or losing? What if we weren't focused on getting more, hitting a stretch goal, or adding to our bottom line?

What if we flipped the goal and made it about increasing the gain for everyone involved. What if we were trying to build value across all our relationships? Would that change our view of the interaction?

A student in one of my classes sold sand. Really, sand. She talked about it in class a lot. She was a good student, focused on getting as much as she could out of the interaction for her company, but also hitting her own goals so that she could maximize her own outcomes. But she often lamented, *sand was sand.* There was no way to add value or differentiate her product. Sure, she could differentiate her company, but if the focus was on the product or the company, sand was sand, a commodity. That makes it a price-only negotiation. Typically, this meant a bid process to see who could provide the cheapest sand. In a bid situation, everyone loses. My student loses the business if she bids too high. If she bids too low, she may get the business but at a financial loss to her company, losing again. The purchaser may think they are winning by getting the lowest price, but in reality, the company that wins the bid doesn't want to provide the best product or the best service unless they can make some money. And it's not a long-term strategy.

During a break in class, I asked her more about the sand. There wasn't more. I asked her about her company. Nothing earth-shattering. What do your customers use the sand for, I asked, grasping for something.

Fracking.

Now, in Texas, we know about getting oil out of the ground. This is big business, and there are complex relationships at work. There is a lot that needs to happen to go from the engineering stage to actual extraction. While I don't know all those stages, I know that it's difficult and sometimes dangerous work.

And it's work completed by people. And people want to do business with other people that they trust, especially when livelihood and safety are on the line.

We talked for the whole break and after class about developing that relationship and developing the idea that even though fracking can happen with *any* sand, the process can't happen *without* sand. And if the whole process can break without this one component, it must be a pretty important component. This takes sand out of the commodity column. It is still substitutable, but it is no longer viewed as a less important part of the process. In fact, it is a critical part of the process, because the process can't happen without it. If you can't complete the fracking process without sand, it becomes mission critical.

This reframing moves my sand-selling student out of the position of losing if she bids too high and losing if she bids too low. The shift in focus is not about selling or buying but a reward structure. If the organization shifts its focus to a reward structure, the student can shift her goals to developing relationships. It means she and the company can expand the available outcomes.

The question is whether you view the world as a world of munificence or a world of scarcity. This small difference in mindset can mean everything in your everyday interactions.

The scarcity viewpoint looks at every interaction as a division of scarce resources. If you believe scarcity is the state of the world, you believe that there are limited resources. You believe that resources are so limited that any resources that other parties get in a negotiation come directly out of your share. The scarcity mindset is very positional. This means that they enter into the negotiation or interaction with a predetermined idea about what can be accomplished, about how they get the outcome they desire, and are blind to different outcomes that achieve their goal.

Scarcity limits your thinking. In a scarcity mindset, you become positional because you are trying to defend that outcome. You are trying to protect your limited, biased view of the best outcome. The assumption in the scarcity mindset is that you alone can uncover the value in the interaction, whether you explicitly state that or consciously think it. By holding fast to the idea that your position is the only way to achieve your outcome, you reject the views and creativity of the other parties involved.

Scarcity invokes an emotional reaction. Scarcity invokes fear. And fear changes our outlook on the situation. When we experience negative emotions, it impacts how we process information. When we experience fear, we get defensive, we get positional. Positional negotiators are unwilling to give up on the offers or concessions that they have given. They stick by the number that they predetermined before the negotiation.

And you're probably thinking, *Great! I want people in my organization to be tough negotiators.*

I agree. We want people to be tough negotiators. I want to be tough; I want others with whom I'm negotiating to be tough. That's right. I want my "adversary" to be tough.

Tough doesn't mean positional. Tough doesn't mean hard-headed. And tough doesn't mean that you try to win. Even more so, tough doesn't mean that you are trying not to lose.

We spend too much time defining areas of our life in terms of winning or losing. Most of our lives are outside of that convention.

The idea of munificence is a view that the world contains lavish resources beyond what we can see or grasp within the frame of our immediate control. This view sees interactions as a way to leverage that excess and to gain. A key difference between munificence and optimism is that the optimist may think an interaction will go her way and she will get some gain in that interaction, while someone who is focused on a munificent worldview sees the interaction as a possibility for great gain—for all involved. That is, the munificent worldview doesn't think there is a constrained amount of resources being distributed. The munificent worldview sees the interaction as a way to discover what lavish resources can be uncovered and shared.

We need to adopt a munificent worldview to find and maximize our potential outcomes.

Business is not a game. Business is not a win-lose proposition. If we adopt a win-lose perspective on our interactions, we are embracing a view of the interaction and of the world that is limited. The assumption is that of a competition. The assumption is that one can't win unless someone else loses. Even if you profess a win-win ideology, the term win itself implies a loser. When we use the rhetoric of "win" on any level, it activates in our mind the limited idea of winning and losing. According to Luke 18:14: "Everyone who exalts himself will be humbled, and he who humbles himself will be exalted."

This idea—whether it is openly approached as a competitive situation or covertly acted upon as a competitive situation—changes our interactions. Approaching negotiations with a motive to win or not lose impacts several different aspects of the interaction.

Including losing in the interaction brings a number of problems to the table. These are the problems that we often associate with negotiation, the reasons many people don't like to negotiate. Once we determine that our interactions include a loser or losers, we are also including three specific problems. We are introducing relationship damage, we are negatively impacting trust, and we are imposing false outcomes on either the interaction or the organization.

Relationship Damage

Everyone has been in those relationships that are somewhat frustrating. We have that one individual in our department, that person in our family, that friend, who always seems to get just what they want. It's not a bad thing, unless we see that this individual is gaining while we lose. If the favored person in your department consistently gets the best assignments, the lion's share of the budget, or the best customers it can be frustrating, especially if you end up taking less than the best.

It becomes an organizational justice question. When different parties start to weigh the outcomes and measure the outcomes, it becomes a problem. When the different parties to the negotiation are stuck in the thought process of working out who got how much, you know you are in a situation with a party that will be a loser. Remember what Proverbs 16:8 says: "Better is little with righteousness, than vast revenues without justice."

While these interactions are becoming fewer, they do exist. We do find ourselves in zero-sum interactions on occasion. Sometimes we win, sometimes we lose. The best way to manage these interactions is to try and be as equitable as possible so that the party with the losing outcome doesn't focus on that losing outcome. Additionally, we need to be sure that we are treating all parties with dignity and respect. We know that the research supports the power of treating people with dignity and respect. If our interactions are zero-sum but we treat people in a manner that provides dignity and respect, they are more likely to adhere to the agreed upon outcome. They are more likely to return to negotiate again, and they are more likely to recommend the interaction to others.

All of this is good to know, but there is another important consideration. If we are involved in interactions with winners and losers—zero-sum interactions—we need to be sure that the same party doesn't end up on the losing side all the time.

By allowing one party to absorb the negative outcome on multiple occasions, we place that party in a situation that demands attention. It demands action. It demands that the relationship be severed, it demands that the losing party make attempts to remedy that situation. It often will produce some defensiveness, dirty tricks, or even methods that may be unethical to try and even the balance.

However, if we work toward benefiting both parties in these interactions, we can keep the outcomes more evenly balanced. This is how a zero-sum negotiation can become a joint gain interaction. But it takes a commitment from parties that care about each other to ensure this works. More about this in a later chapter.

Negatively Impacting Trust

Think about relationships that you have that are, or that could be, lopsided. In those relationships, it seems that in every interaction there's always one party that comes out on top. Now, do you trust that party?

Trust comes from a sense of knowing the reaction that someone will have to an interaction. If I put myself in a vulnerable position, and we have had some previous dealings, I base the likelihood of a potential outcome on the previous outcomes. We don't really go through a conscious look at the possibilities and the outcomes, but rather this process happens as part of heuristic decision making.

Heuristic decision making is a process of shortcutting the decision. If we have experience with a decision, if we have information that we believe, or if we been through a similar situation, we make an assumption that the current interaction will go the same way. If we have had positive interactions with an organization in the past, we assume the next interaction will be positive. It's fairly easy to perpetuate a positive relationship. It's also fairly easy to destroy trust by not maintaining consistency in the relationship.

False or Constrained Outcomes

When I view the world with a scarcity viewpoint, I limit the potential outcomes that I can achieve. I limit the size and the variety of outcomes, and I force every participant in the negotiation into these constraints.

Are there any positives to this win-win, zero-sum view of our interactions? There must be; why else would it be the dominant idea in negotiation? We are all looking for an easy way to quantify our day. Did we win or lose? Did we achieve what we were trying to achieve? This is an easy way to look at our negotiation interactions. How close did we come to our preconceived idea of a good outcome? How many concessions did we have to give? Did the other parties look miserable when they walked out? If they did, we probably won.

That's how our thinking goes. We look for confirming evidence that we did ok in the interaction.

Competitive negotiation doesn't lead to success. In fact, it leads to negative outcomes for those who adopt it.

It assumes a zero-sum negotiation.

It splits resources. It doesn't create resources.

It is positional, limited, and not creative.

The biggest problem is that competitive negotiation creates a loser. There is always at least one party who loses, and typically, there is more than one party who loses.

Creating a loser when it's not a necessary condition is the biggest problem in a competitive negotiation.

It creates a rift in the relationship.

It negatively impacts interdependence.

It negatively impacts the available resources.

And it negatively impacts the outcomes.

When we live in a world that is focused on wins and losses, as described in the first two chapters, it impacts the way that we approach everyday life. It dulls us to the consistent choices that we make that are actually moral dilemmas.

A moral dilemma in negotiation is making a choice between putting people first or putting profit first. It's all-or-nothing thinking. I know many sales organizations that fall prey to this thought process. I've had goals that are only focused on hitting a quota—many of us have been in this position. Or maybe you're a writer and you are focused on click throughs, or any number of other professions that focus on the tangible, countable outcomes that don't necessarily serve others. All or nothing.

All or nothing thinking is a cover-up for fear and shame.

A moral dilemma, as defined by the current thinking in philosophy, occurs when there is a decision that must be made between two different choices, each of which is suboptimal. This means that choosing one of the options necessitates losing out on the benefits of the other option. Very often, when we negotiate, we are put in a position that necessitates a false choice. This is a view of our interactions that is born from a scarcity mindset.

This scarcity mindset view of the world maintains that resources are limited, and in order for someone to gain, someone else has to give up

chapter 3

THE MORAL DILEMMA (PEOPLE VS. PROFIT)

resources. This is the basis for a lot of negotiation and sales training courses and books. It's an outdated view that we embrace because of the fear and shame that comes with being "unsuccessful."

I'm trying to be nice with my words. There is a fear that we will be the loser in the interaction. It's a real fear. Losing usually has consequences. Lose enough sales and you get fired. Lose enough in any metric that your organization measures and there will be repercussions. Lose enough in your relationships and that leads to shame. The shame of being at the bottom of your field. The shame of being surpassed by your peers, the shame of losing the respect of your family.

A moral dilemma exists when there is a choice between people and profits. It's a common occurrence in daily life. Profits are our gains. They can be the monetary outcome or some other tangible benefit, but they can also be an intangible outcome, something else we desire. It could be fame, it could be recognition, reputation—anything that is a benefit.

Understand, it's not the benefit itself that's bad. It's the priority. It's the motivation. The hard part is that the motive and the priority in our interactions is hidden. It can't be seen and expressed, but is only really known by the one who holds that motive, that priority.

What causes us to prioritize outcomes over people? Fear. And shame.

You've seen these choices in your daily life. Maybe you make a choice in traffic to cut someone off so that you can get ahead of them, rather than slowing down to get in the lane behind them. We see moving ahead of someone as an advantage. We want to win, and we put our win ahead of the people on the road.

Or maybe this happens when someone gives you too much change after a purchase. An unbalanced register for a clerk is probably a bigger deal than that extra dollar or two. But often, we walk away with the change.

It's easy to give that change back because the benefit is small. But what happens when the stakes are much larger? What happens when your job depends on this? Are you willing to put the people before the profit in that case?

How does this work for the salesperson who needs to hit her quota to be promoted? How about if she needs to hit the quota to keep her job? What are the different implications to the individual versus the organization?

Only through loving our fellow man can we get through this fear. "There is no fear in love, but perfect love casts out fear. For fear has to do with punishment, and whoever fears has not been perfected in love." (1 John 4:18)

Inexperienced negotiators view the interaction in terms of an objective right or wrong. Moreover, they measure outcomes on the basis of right or wrong. This can lead to a situation that extrapolates from right and wrong, to good and bad, leading these inexperienced negotiators down a path that can incorrectly categorize an outcome that should be quantified as a gain. But if this outcome doesn't meet a predetermined ideal, it may be dismissed as a "bad" outcome. (Most of the time we call this a loss.)

Negotiation, as defined by Lax and Sebenius (1986), is a process where parties in apparent conflict seek to achieve better outcomes through jointly decided actions. Within this arena of strategic interactions, the ethical underpinning plays a crucial role, one that is deeply intertwined with our moral compass and principles. Since this is a joint decision, rather than an individual decision, or multiple individual decisions, there is a potential for manipulation or deceit. Some individuals see this opportunity for deceit as the opportunity to gain advantage. It is not.

It is essential to acknowledge that deceit can often creep into competitive negotiations, as noted by Lewicki and Hiam (2006).

The Bible's wisdom, particularly in Proverbs 17:4, warns that wicked individuals lend an ear to evil lips and pay heed to malicious tongues. This cautionary verse reminds us of the moral pitfalls of deception, a path fraught with ethical dilemmas. Rather, we are meant to value and even to love those with whom our paths cross. If we enter a negotiation with a posture of love for the others involved, it makes it much more difficult to deceive them. When you interact with your closest family, do you deceive them? And if you are deceiving them, are you showing love? Of course not. In deception you are putting yourself, or your feelings, ahead of theirs.

Proverbs 19:22 reinforces the importance of honesty by stating that it is better to be poor than to be a liar. The Bible underscores that financial gain achieved through dishonesty is unsustainable. Dishonest money dwindles away, as Proverbs 13:11 advises, while those who accumulate wealth honestly see it grow little by little.

Thompson (2009) emphasizes how lying in negotiation compresses or reduces the bargaining zone and can adversely affect offers and concessions. In contrast, collaborative dealmaking thrives on the honest sharing of interests and the strategic and deliberate sharing of positions, as highlighted by Lewicki and Hiam (2006). Such collaboration turns the negotiation into a puzzle that should be solved collectively, aligning with the notion that parties should benefit each other as a means of benefiting themselves.

In the realm of negotiation, ethics and morality should guide our actions, in line with biblical wisdom. A hot-tempered approach, as cautioned in Proverbs 19:19, can lead to undesirable consequences. It's also vital to avoid controversies, strife, and malicious talk, as outlined in I Timothy 6:4-6. Instead, one should prioritize Godliness with contentment over financial gain.

Envy, a corrosive emotion, can drive individuals to deceive their counterparts, as indicated by Moran and Schweitzer (2005). However, those who maintain a cooperative demeanor, even when negotiating with highly competitive individuals, can extract more value, as Banas and McLean-Parks (2002) suggest, "The meek may not inherit the earth, but they get more out of the negotiation," a sentiment that is definitely in line with Jesus's words in Matthew.

There is an assumption that all negotiations are competitive. Rather, parties should benefit themselves by benefiting the other party. Negotiation is not just a strategic game of conflicting interests but also a moral and ethical exercise. It challenges us to adhere to principles of honesty, cooperation, and contentment as we navigate through the complex terrain of dealmaking. In the end, true success in negotiation lies not just in financial gain but in the harmony between ethical conduct and achieving mutually beneficial outcomes.

The reality is that the moral dilemma doesn't exist as a true dichotomy of one choice over the other. What happens is a decision on a sliding scale between the options. And oftentimes the scales that we slide along are much more than an easy choice of two.

We make the decision in our lives about whether we should accept an assignment at work and that negotiation involves several parties. We need to balance the scales in this dilemma between the wishes of our superiors, peers, and team members. Additionally, there are constituencies at home with an interest in the outcome—a spouse or partner, children, parents who are being cared for, friends, clubs, church groups, etc.

When we make the decision between the potential profit to the organization, our superiors, ourselves, and the people involved—family, friends, ourselves—it is not an easy black and white choice. But most of the time, the moral dilemma is a false dichotomy.

Wait? The moral dilemma isn't really a dilemma.

We often approach morals as a choice in our interactions. Sometimes we do this consciously, but most of the time this is an unconscious application of a bias. The bias may be an indicator of what we inherently value, but more likely it's something more than that influencing our choices. What is probably happening is that misaligned organizational goals are leading us to this false dichotomy.

This is one of the most common discussions that I have with my Executive students, whether they are in an MBA program or in an executive training session. They want to be able to work with people. They see the value of relationships. They recognize the utility in trust. And they have organizational goals that put them in a position to make a choice. These are organizational goals that pit their value for the human component against their value for the organization's (or their own) profit goals.

A moral dilemma means we're going to have to make a choice between two outcomes or two paths, either of which could be a good path, but by choosing one path we are choosing to eschew the other.

What we typically want to do when we're faced with a moral dilemma is have a set of values, a set of morals, that we can call on so we can make the decision on the spot. This is not something that is new to decision-makers. It is not something that is new to the world that we live in; this happens pretty consistently.

We see this quite a bit in our day-to-day lives. Let me give you a couple of organizational stories that may help you understand better. One of the companies I worked for opened a sales office, and I was the manager. We struggled when we opened because the organization was not well known. We were trying to develop sales, to build some momentum. I was tasked with hiring and training salespeople. One of my hires had a lot of promise. She was very highly sought after, and we were lucky to get her. She worked for a month in the sales office and then went to the Home Office for some training.

While she was at the Home Office she called me and told me that her significant other had received a job offer on the other side of the country and she would be moving soon. She wanted to know what the best course of action was and how she should proceed with training. She was a couple of days into a two-week training program. It was an expensive two-week training paid for out of the budget from my struggling sales branch.

I had to decide about whether we should keep her as an employee. Should we put the money into training and developing her as a salesperson knowing that within a month or two months she would be moving and leaving our branch? Should we continue paying to develop her as a salesperson or should we cut her loose? This was a difficult decision that I was not comfortable making. The decision would have a big impact on this person's life. I was determining her livelihood—making the decision between people or profit in an organization that was working to grow. Cutting costs was very desirable, and thus, this decision had to be weighed seriously.

What should I do? I could help her develop and move on. I could help her become better, even more desirable for the next organization that will take her on, or I could cut my costs and improve my performance, which would impact my own compensation. It was a moral dilemma. It wasn't easy as I negotiated over the phone with her.

I was part of yet another organization, a small startup that we were establishing from scratch. We were utilizing technology licensed from a university to develop it into a software product. The founders brought in a new CEO who was very concerned with productivity, specifically with sales. The venture capital investors were focused on the business's cash flow.

One of the founders of the company, who was a software engineer, took on building a new revenue stream for the company selling services around the use of the software. He voluntarily moved into a sales role, out of his comfort zone, to try and benefit the company. In the weekly sales meeting, everyone who was responsible for a revenue stream had to go around the table and report their quota achievement. When it came to the nascent services business, the company's founder did not have a very good first month. Only a month into the quarter, only a month into this new business, and he was way behind his quota.

The CEO had to decide whether he was going to sanction one of the founders of the organization or give some grace. Would he give some opportunity to build this fledgling part of the business? Typically, if you were way behind the quota, you were publicly reprimanded by the CEO. You may be put on a developmental program. It would cost you some dollars in your paycheck. Since this was a founder who was trying to build an entirely new aspect of the business, most around the table assumed there would be some grace. Afterall, he was only a month into this new revenue stream. The quota was a guess since it was a new business. But we knew the CEO and waited around the table as we watched him get angrier at the report of the lackluster services sales. It was a very public moral dilemma.

The fact is, there are no right or wrong answers for each of these situations. They are dilemmas.

In the first, I had to call my area manager and ask him what I should do about this new sales rep that was already planning on moving. His recommendation was to cut her loose. To fire her immediately. The Human Resources Department had a different recommendation. They said we should give her the time. Give her the development and if she decides to move on, she'll move with an expanded skill set. It was a difficult decision because it impacted the profitability of my branch negatively, which impacted my compensation and my area manager's compensation negatively. We let her continue the training. She left the company three weeks after returning from the training.

In the second example, I sat at the table when the CEO fired the quota-struggling founder of the company. He told him it was time to move on. "If you can't build this services business in the first month, and you're one of the developers of the code, you never will." Fired on the spot.

Each of these scenarios provides a difficult decision in the face of a moral dilemma. How do you make those decisions with limited information?

I can give you some ideas about how to address these dilemmas, but in reality, it comes down to consistency. Consistency with our morals, consistency with our values, consistency in our decision-making.

In addition to consistency, we need integrity. Typically, when I teach this in a classroom setting, we discuss integrity and its formation. But we can't have that discussion here. Integrity means, "Am I applying a standard?" Integrity is about having a set of values and morals that are consistently applied. So, my integrity could be based on applying a set of twisted morals.

This is where the rubber meets the road. This is an important decision that will follow you and will impact your relationships, trust, and reputation. So, which standard will you use? The standard that says, "It's business. And in business, you must do what you have to do." Or will you use a different standard? One that sets you apart from the typical?

In 1 Peter 3 verse 10, the apostle tells us that "The one who desires life, to love and see good days, must keep his tongue from evil and his lips from speaking deceit." Peter doesn't say, keep your lips from speaking deceit unless you need to shade the truth a little to make that big sale. He's clear. If you want life, love, and good days, have a standard that doesn't include decisions that you need to justify.

Don't hear me saying to embrace naïveté. No, in fact, I'm saying you need to be better, smarter, and work harder to uphold your Christian integrity. Jesus tells his disciples that they need to be "shrewd as serpents" when dealing with the wolves in the world. But he also cautioned them to be as "innocent as doves" in the same verse (Matthew 10:16). We are called as negotiators to be shrewd and to be innocent. We are called to be tough negotiators who are also blameless in our interactions.

I know you don't want others to take advantage of you in your interactions. But what is it that makes you think that being innocent means others will take advantage of you? I know it's a real fear, but why? This book is built to address that question. People who are prepared and understand how negotiation works won't be susceptible to tactics that take advantage of them.

For those who understand negotiation at a deeper level, the moral dilemma becomes easier to understand, and decisions are, therefore, easier to make. If I look back at my sales rep, who may leave, my decision becomes less about, "Is she trying to take advantage of me? Is this going to negatively impact my bottom line this month?" And it becomes a decision about, "Who do I want to be as a boss? Who do I want to be as a mentor to my *remaining* sales reps? What image do I want for my branch, my people, my organization in the community?" This is an easier question to answer. The volume of the dilemma gets turned down, and I can make a decision that fits me and who I am as a negotiator.

It becomes a decision about values.

> *"For of this you can be sure: No immoral, impure or greedy person—such a person is an idolater—has any inheritance in the kingdom of Christ and of God. Let no one deceive you with empty words, for because of such things God's wrath comes on those who are disobedient. Therefore do not be partners with them. For you were once darkness, but now you are light in the Lord. Live as children of light (for the fruit of the light consists in all goodness, righteousness and truth) and find out what pleases the Lord. Have nothing to do with the fruitless deeds of darkness, but rather expose them"* (Ephesians 5:5-11 [NIV]).

You can see there is a real decision to make. Paul is clear about how to interact with these people. He says, "…do not be partners with them…" but we should live in the light and "have nothing to do with the fruitless deeds of darkness." Those fruitless deeds are the lies and manipulations that we defend under the flag of "It's only business."

And I am telling you, it's indefensible.

This is not a short-term solution to the interaction. This is a long-term, values-based decision. But it's an easy decision to get wrong. And I did get it wrong. I listened to my boss, my area manager, and I fired that sales rep. She was back at her hotel room packing to go home when the Vice President of Human Resources found her and told her that she wasn't fired. He told her that wasn't how this company did business. I was wrong. And I had to go to the home office and sit with my bosses to explain myself. They were gracious and understood my short-sighted position. It helped that my boss had told me to fire her. I was sent home with some strong words about the values of the organization and the open-door policy of the upper management if I had questions.

My boss wasn't treated as gently. He had a history of rash decisions. He was moved out of the Area Manager job soon after and was put in another position. One that had far less decision-making power. He left the company not long after. I don't know if he left on his own or if he was asked to leave. I do know his values didn't match up with the organization's values. Part of that was personality, but the organization isn't blameless in this either. The goals that we had as Branch Managers and Area Managers supported the short-term, win-the-sale-at-all-costs viewpoints.

And this is the dilemma that many of you face. Are you negotiating for the goals of the organization to the detriment of your own goals? Or worse, to the detriment of your own value structure?

Is there a way to maximize your gain, the gain for the organization, the gain for the others involved in the negotiation, *and* maintain your own integrity? Or is that just a misinformed dream?

This is where we fall into the dilemma. No one would choose to do something in a negotiation that harms others. (Well, most wouldn't.) But when faced with the difficult choice because of misaligned goals, it becomes much more likely.

We must make these decisions with integrity. That means, before my negotiation I need to understand my morals and values. I need to go into the negotiation and know what I'm going to value most.

In the first situation, where I've got a sales rep who has told me she will likely move on in two months, I must think about what is most important to me, not just from a short-term, zero-sum standpoint. How will this impact my reputation? My business? My bottom line? All these things come into play when we are making our decision. I'm not saying this is an easy decision. What I'm saying is we need to weigh this and really look at what's most important.

My area manager was compensated based on the profitability of the five sales branches in his charge. If he has a branch that's leaking money because we're paying to train somebody who's never going to be a productive sales professional, that's a negative for his individual goals. He told me to fire her because that was the right thing for him and his short-term compensation plan. His organizational outcomes supported this decision.

Human Resources should protect both the organization's reputation and the people within the organization. There is also a legal aspect that needs to be considered. Human Resources has a different view of this issue, but they also don't have the same goals or metrics attached to the outcome. Human Resources has goals to train individuals in the company. I don't know if there was any compensation connected with this goal.

However, HR was located at the organization's home office. The executives had daily contact with the department members. Those of us in the sales offices did not have daily contact with the executives or even the home office. The culture was determined by each manager's interpretation of the organization's goals for salespeople.

If you are unclear about your values, you make the decision based on short-term goals.

> *"Do nothing from selfish ambition or conceit, but in humility count others more significant than yourselves. Let each of you look not only to his own interests, but also to the interests of others. Have this mind among yourselves, which is yours in Christ Jesus"* (Philippians 2:3-5).

To let this sales rep continue the training program impacted my compensation negatively, it impacted my area manager's compensation negatively, but it was an important long-term goal for the organization. The organization was founded on principles that were focused on employee success, positive culture and environment, and concern for the human aspects of business. The culture allowed for flexibility in work, we had dogs in the offices, we had an informal gathering every Friday, during the workday, to unwind and enjoy—we had beer and snacks. The executives didn't want a cutthroat environment, but the organizational goals didn't align with that idea.

We needed to remedy that situation. Had I been open with my area manager, and had he been open with the people at the home office about how this dilemma affected us, we could have made a decision that made sense for everyone.

And that is what the science would support as well. I'm not arguing here to give up your compensation because that's the "Christian thing" to do. I'm writing this book to refute the thinking that there is a cost to doing business in a way that is God-pleasing. It is not a dichotomous choice.

Think about other negotiations. Should I pit two suppliers against one another? If I bid this project to everyone, will I get a lower price? If I ask this recent college grad what her salary requirements are, will I be able to pay her less because she doesn't know how to answer that question?

The question you should ask yourself is, how do I want to measure success?

Do you want to measure how much you can dominate the others involved in the negotiation?

Do you want to measure if you achieved the positions that you brought into the interaction?

Or do you want to measure the overall gain in the interaction?

When I teach this, especially to MBA students, there is a lot of doubt. People see this as giving up power in the negotiation. We'll get into some deeper ideas of power in a later chapter, but for now, I want you to think about power a little differently. Let's define power not as getting what we want but as creating the most value.

A lot of negotiation books and training focus on getting people to give you what you want from the interaction. Honestly, you can get what you want without negotiating. If you use leverage or manipulation, you can push people into your outcome.

But if you are here to get the most from your interdependent relationships, you need to think bigger.

Each person in an interdependent relationship brings unique

value—that's the definition of interdependence. If you don't open yourself up to this value, you miss out on potential. What you bring to the negotiation is a limited, biased view of the potential outcomes. You don't have all the information. You don't hold all the value. If you do hold all the value, stop negotiating.

There isn't a reason to negotiate if you don't add value by adding parties to the interaction.

But, if you realize that others bring unique value to the interaction, then you also need to accept that they may have some ideas about ways to unlock that value. Maybe you have not thought of all the ideas; maybe you aren't all-knowing. Maybe we need each other.

The research says that people added to an interaction bring unique value. It is the job of the expert negotiator to maximize this value. Often, when we are deep in the interaction, our focus narrows. We get myopic and attend only to our own positions. That's what leads to competitive, zero-sum interactions. This is why the research points out that many interactions that have potential for gain fall short of that potential.

A former student, Fernando, had a summer internship at Dell in Austin. Fernando is an older MBA student. He has a family. This makes taking a two-month position that's almost a hundred miles away from his home difficult. But Dell does this a lot, so they have some intern housing. He moved, with his family, to Austin for the summer.

His job was developing a plan of action in the Dell cybersecurity division. Some internship projects that companies use are very exploratory in nature, and some are very instrumental or applied. This project was a combination. Fernando, particularly his experience in relationship building, made great strides in the project.

This isn't an earth-shattering breakthrough story—the student goes on an internship, performs well, and expects to be offered a position.

It's bigger than that.

Fernando's wife had a career in the city where they lived, and his kids had connections at schools. So, uprooting for a summer was difficult but not impossible. Uprooting forever was a big change and one that he hadn't considered a possibility.

Summer ended, and it was time for interns to present their work. After the presentations, the meetings with department heads happened. That's when jobs are offered, and career trajectory is determined. Fernando's presentation went well. He achieved quite a lot over the summer, but the expectations were high. After his presentation, he was asked to meet with some individuals that he'd

chapter 4

WHAT DO YOU (REALLY) WANT?

worked with over the summer and the head of the cybersecurity department. It was a big deal. And there was a catch. They were to meet and play golf. *Great,* you might be saying, that sounds relaxed and fun. Unless you have never played golf before, and Fernando had not.

We have all been in situations like this—a foreign experience that is competitive, and the stakes are high.

"What did you do...?" I asked, on the edge of my seat.

"I had a great discussion with the head of cyber security." He answered.

Brilliant. Fernando approached the experience at an interest level. The golf game was irrelevant to him. The game was simply a context. But that competitive context didn't drive Fernando to try to win, hit long drives, or even play well. He explained that he had never golfed before, but he was interested and excited to try. Then, he proceeded to focus on the important aspect of the meeting, which was the relationship development.

It's not surprising that Dell made him an offer for full-time employment to start at the end of his MBA studies. They asked him what he needed in a salary and benefits package to take the job. Fernando knew that he was in a good position, so he asked for his aspirational package. He wanted his interests met as close to perfectly as possible, and he wanted to work remote. Rather than picking up and moving his family, he wanted the company to facilitate a remote working position. He asked for it all.

Dell said no.

The salary that he asked for was outside of the range they paid newly minted MBAs. He had gone too far. Everything else was doable, but this one positional item pushed him over the limit with Dell.

But that isn't the end of the story because Fernando is not a positional bargainer. For most people who think positionally, this would be the end. But for Fernando—he asked them the big question: Why? Why is what I requested beyond the limit? They explained that the "typical" hire that they make has very little experience in the business world. Dell needs to make a big commitment to develop these individuals.

If you remember, Fernando is not the typical MBA student with two years of low-level experience. He was an older student with a lot of relevant experience, and he let them know.

He challenged their standard—in a positive way. After considering his defense of his offer, they accepted it. He maintained his interests. He focused on what was important to him. He was willing to walk away if his interests couldn't be met. And he was willing to articulate those interests to the other parties involved.

This only worked because he had shown the company the value he would bring to the interaction. He had a successful project over the summer, including implementing it. He interacted in a difficult, foreign situation and was able to maintain that interest focus. He brought value to the interaction but was unwilling to settle in the negotiation for less than his value. And he got his value.

That's the power of being focused on interests.

If he had been focused on the position in the negotiation, he may have tried to split the difference on the salary number; he may have caved to their standard, thinking he could work for raises in the future. His interests wouldn't have been met, and eventually, it would have impacted the relationship.

> "*And the effect of righteousness will be peace and the result of righteousness, quietness and trust forever*" (Isaiah 32:17).

I live in an incredibly Christian-skewed community. The people that I'm around all day, the people I see, the people that I work with, they're mostly Christian in background. I have to say, it's a very difficult situation sometimes. The quote from Isaiah above is revealing to me. As Christians, we talk about righteousness. We assume that doing business with another "Christian businessperson" will make everything easier. *Of course they will treat me right.*

But the reality of this quote is that one must be righteous and in the presence of righteousness in order to experience quietness and trust. That is not going to happen for you in this part of your eternal life. Isaiah is pointing to the return of Christ when all the righteous will be gathered and live in quietness and trust.

The world we live in is broken. We can't depend on righteousness, quietness, or trust. In fact, what I have seen over a decade and a half of teaching executives is that trust is nearly nonexistent. Rather than trust, we have business dealings that are filled with suspicion. Businesses are loaded down with lawyers and contracts. Positve interactions between individuals are nearly impossible to achieve because of the fear that someone will take advantage of you. We all feel it.

There is another way, and it's a better way. I'm writing this to open your eyes to it. It's not an easier way, I'm going to be honest. The easy way is to just keep doing what you're doing, to embrace the world and what the world puts out as the way that business is done. But that's not what we are called to do. We are called to do things the hard way. Christians are called to more.

> "This is my commandment, that you love one another as I have
> loved you." (John 15:12)

Notice here that Jesus doesn't say, "Love one another, but business is business." We know that when confronted with unethical business practices, Jesus is willing to stand up, fashion a whip out of cords, and overturn tables. Jesus doesn't think that it's only business, that if you *can* charge a high price for pigeons because people have a spiritual need for pigeons it's okay to run your business that way. It's not ok.

One constant in business today is that most do not perceive their approach to business as righteous. Churches, my Christian university, technology businesses, oil and gas, services, everywhere that I am exposed, I see people making choices under the banner that reads, "It's just business."

I have wondered about this for a long time. Why do people apply different morals in the context of business than they do in their personal life? Most of us wouldn't teach our children to lie but have no problem telling a supplier, "We just don't have the budget for that. You need to lower your price," when it isn't the truth. The truth a lot of times, is "We just don't care if you make a profit and are able to feed and take care of your families. We care about our profit." Or maybe, "We're really selfish. We'd really like that big house and new car and we're willing to get it at your expense." That is really what we mean when we utter the phrase—it's just business; it's the way business works.

I am the first to admit I have been cornered by this. I imagine you have also felt this pressure. I was sitting with a friend, having lunch. We were talking about similar situations. He described this as being stuck between the Red Sea and Pharoah's army. Apply that phrase to your business life. Are you stuck between doing the things that the world teaches to get more and your own morality and values? Do you have to make an ethical choice that you don't like?

I felt called to write this book. It is my current ethical choice. I know the reward for this book at my institution will be small. As a professor in a university, my reward is based on peer-reviewed publication. If I followed the rewards system I would conduct a research study and write it for publication in an academic journal. My university would benefit. But you would never read it. You would never learn from it.

If I wrote for an academic journal, I wouldn't be able to approach the subject in the way that I feel called to write about it—I would be trapped between the Red Sea and Pharaoh's army. Or, as I said to my friend, "I feel like I'm waiting to be swallowed by a fish."

God called Jonah in the Old Testament to go to Nineveh and alert them that their sinful way of life had not gone unnoticed. Jonah, not a big fan of the Ninevites, had other plans. He ran from God's calling. His method of escaping God was to board a ship and get as far away from the presence of God as he could. We can't really fault Jonah because many of us do this every day in the way we treat others, again, under the banner of business. We don't try to understand and help our employees. We set goals and use those as a strict guideline. We put ourselves between the Red Sea of employee performance and Pharoah's army of employee discipline. There is a choice. There is another way, and it is God's way.

The people of Israel, who were fleeing slavery, trapped between the Red Sea and Pharaoh's army, gave up hope. They grumbled to Moses about their perceived choices, dying in the desert or living comfortable lives as slaves.

Jonah had a similar dilemma: either run away from God or go tell the people in the big, powerful city of Nineveh that they were sinning and God would bring judgment. Again, God showed up and said stop boxing yourself in. There's another way.

In both cases, there was a third way out—the creative solution. The caveat to the creative solution? Trust God. The Israelites walked through a parted Red Sea to safety. Jonah was swallowed by a fish and regurgitated three days later.

And so, my friend and I sat at lunch and complained about the Christian organizations we worked for, him trapped between the Red Sea and Pharaoh's army and me waiting to be swallowed by a fish. But, as I thought about it more, I realized we, all of us Christians, are already swallowed by the fish. We are standing in the middle of the Red Sea, and just like Jonah and the people of Israel, we have a choice to make. Jonah's time in the fish was a time of prayer and reflection about how he was dealing with people. His relationship with the Ninevites was under examination. He didn't go to represent God because he didn't like them. Ever been in that situation, treating someone differently because you don't really like them? It's easy to be nice to the people in the pews at church on Sunday, but what about the person who cuts you off in traffic? What about the customer who is angry? What about the boss who disrespects you and treats you unfairly?

I find myself in this situation with my boss right now. I don't like him, and he doesn't like me. I am Jonah. I have to understand that the perspective I hold is my reality, not his reality. From his perspective, I'm Nineveh. The point is we don't like each other. I don't want to treat him better than he treats me. There is some excellent research showing that when we are faced with a negative emotional state, we change our goals. Rather than focusing on accomplishing our objective, we change the goal to retaliation and punishment of the party with whom we are interacting. So, I'm Jonah. I don't like my Ninevite boss, and I want to see God's punishment rain down on him.

I have been waiting for the fish to swallow me.

But, I realize, I've already been swallowed by this fish. I'm not waiting for the crew to pitch me into the sea. I'm in the fish. The circumstances that I have allowed in my daily interactions have put me in the position of being swallowed. I'm in the fish. And in case you missed it, you are in the fish as well. You are swallowed up by the circumstances of living in a broken world. The slights that you have faced have built you up to protect yourself. You worry about protecting your position, your outcome. Every interaction is shaded with suspicion.

Understand this—Jonah saw two choices: love the Ninevites or run from God. But God gave him a third choice.

Every day, we interact with people, whether business or personal. We see two ways. I'm basing this on years of research, teaching, and participation in the human interaction we call negotiation. The two ways that we see are winning and losing. You know, win-win. There's the winner and...

The first-place loser?

There is another way. We are not trapped between the Red Sea and Pharaoh's army. This other way is called joint gain. Joint gain isn't focused on me. Joint gain isn't about what I get out of the interaction. But joint gain also isn't about you. It isn't about altruistically giving to another party in the negotiation. Joint gain is focusing on benefitting everyone involved in the interaction. Benefitting them as much as possible.

This idea of joint gain may be new and intriguing to you. Most of the time, when I teach these ideas, my students are very skeptical. How will benefiting the others involved in a negotiation do me any good? Why would I want to help the opponent? My question is, *why are the others with whom you interact your opponents?* Take a minute and reflect on that question. Why do you approach others with whom you do business as the enemy? Wouldn't you want them to help you achieve your goals?

I know what you are thinking: *It's because they treat you like the enemy!* This is a typical human reaction. It's so typical that in the 1960s, Axelrod explained it using game theory. He said we have a game theoretic answer to this idea. When entering an interaction, we should first enter with the idea of cooperating, but if the other party takes advantage of that cooperation, we should retaliate with a competitive move. It's called tit-for-tat. Everyone knows this strategy. The idea makes some sense to people.

However, people are always fearful of the opening move. If I go first and the other party takes advantage of me, will I be able to levy a punishment heavy enough that I can get even? But is that what you want to accomplish in your business negotiations? Making sure you can deal out punishments to people who wrong you?

Pontius Pilate tried this tit-for-tat strategy. Angry at the Jews, who themselves were an angry mob, Pilate offered a cooperative move in his negotiation. He offered Barabbas or Jesus. What an easy choice! Barabbas was a terrorist, a murderer, an awful human being. Jesus was a Rabbi that made Pharisees look stupid. He healed the sick. He loved prostitutes and thieves. He talked to lepers. He was love. Barabbas was hate. The Jews picked Barabbas, and Pilate lost his mind. He started cooperative and was met with a competitive move. He was left with the choice to release an enemy of the state or Jesus. Would he do the logical thing that would make the Jews crazy? Or the illogical thing that would punish them for their stupid choices in the interaction?

We are often put into these moral dilemmas in our business life. We often face decisions that, while not on this scale, are the same decisions. Should I do something distasteful but popular or something that will be really unpopular with people who I'm trying to impress? The easy choice is to do something distasteful, even unethical, rather than face the unpopular decision. The easy choice is to fight, to be inflexible, and to blame the corporate goals or quotas. The hard choice is to be contemplative. The hard choice is to ask why and really listen to the other parties. Jesus did this all the time. His opponents came to him often with a mindset to attack. They asked questions that put him in a bad position. They tried to throw him off his game, to unsettle him. "Jesus, should we pay taxes to the Romans? We hate those guys." Jesus didn't rush in with his position. Instead, he gave them a question: "Hey, Pharisees, what are you really trying to accomplish?" I don't really know how he asked them other than what is recorded in the Bible, but I can imagine Jesus asked it in that manner. A very genuine, "Whose picture is on the money? And… what about what you owe to God? Are you thinking about the long-term goals?"

Imagine if you approached your next negotiation that way. If your reseller came to meet with you and said, "I have to have a bigger discount." Instead of your typical response, "I can't do that, we're already at our maximum discount." Or, "If I do that, you will have to increase the volume of your purchase." you say, "Let's explore the possibility." Whose picture is on your coin?

Can you increase your discount? Maybe. Have you explored the reasoning behind the discount? Ask some questions. "Why do you want a bigger discount? What are you trying to accomplish? I'm your partner, and I want you to be successful, but remember, I'm your partner; you should also want me to be successful. Let's look at the long term."

> "If anyone is inclined to be contentious, we have no such practice, nor do the churches of God" (1 Corinthians 11:16 ESV).

If we don't believe that grace is free, why would we believe that someone would take our best interest into consideration? We think this way because we know what our hearts are capable of. We have been selfish. We have been liars. We have been cheaters, thieves, and untrustworthy. We have been crafty.

"Now the serpent was more crafty than any other beast of the field that the LORD God had made" (Genesis 3:1).

We don't like crafty, and we also often don't like transparency because we feel that everyone else is crafty. We don't share information or resources or benefit others because we don't trust that they will share with or benefit us. In turn, the others in the negotiation don't share information or provide benefits. It's a vicious circle.

So, the question becomes, "Why are you even negotiating?"

If you are just there to fight and scrap and try to take something from someone else, why are you putting yourself in the position of becoming interdependent? That's hard. It's much easier to just a take a position of power. Of course, if you are unwilling to be interdependent, that means you are giving that up in all of your relationships. You can't expect others to give you interdependence if you aren't going to give back interdependence. In that dog-eat-dog world, you set yourself up for those with more power to take from you. And you will take from those who are less powerful than you are, and so on.

Again, a vicious circle.

We have a choice.

Why is it that, in a business setting, many people think the obvious choice is to use people or relationships for selfish gain? Why is it that we focus so much on the competitive aspects of business and relationships? Why is a "win at all costs" mentality so pervasive in business?

The good news is we can choose a better belief system. We can embrace the ideas that Paul writes about.

"For you were called to freedom, brothers. Only do not use your freedom as an opportunity for the flesh, but through love serve one another" (Galatians 5:13 ESV).

It seems strange to think that this is not only an acceptable business trait, but a heralded business trait. We hear things like, "He's a killer." "He can't be beat." "He destroys the competition."

Notice this is a male-centric idea. This is an idea that doesn't translate into the female arena. Women who are aggressive, competitive, self-centered negotiators aren't hailed as great huntresses. They are referred to in less flattering ways. While their male counterparts are celebrated, they are derided and looked down on.

This competitive style of negotiating is focused on the self. It may be, and often is, pursued to the detriment of others and sometimes may even be focused on ways to diminish or hurt the gains of others. It is what we call positional in nature (more on positions later). The competitive negotiator wants to achieve a predetermined outcome that forces everyone involved into his/her idea of an achievement. This is a very short-term idea.

This is a defensive stance from which to negotiate. It's defensive in that the negotiators involved are focused on protecting what they view as a limited or finite outcome. This is why it becomes competitive. Those who view the negotiation as a finite or zero-sum endeavor are focused on maintaining the amount of that finite outcome that they have obtained.

So, why the aversion to collaboration? Or, better, why the attraction to competitive negotiation? This is the real question that we should address. Conventional wisdom says don't give in. Any value that you create belongs to you. You should be focused on hitting your goal, working toward your outcome.

We are afraid that if we let our guard down for one minute, the other parties involved will take advantage of us. This leads us to have guarded interactions. It leads to a focus on positions and a desire to win to cover our own outcomes.

When I present this information to Executive MBA students, they are taken aback. They don't see themselves as afraid. They immediately fall back to the position that this is only business, and in business, one has to be ruthless. "Who will take care of me if I don't?" We have training sessions, we have classes, we have bosses, consultants—all of these voices give us the idea of generating value, but only for ourselves.

I am telling you right now, if this is the way you negotiate, you are weak.

Strong negotiators are willing to be open with their interests. Why? You need to be strong about the reason that you are there to negotiate. You need to stand firm with that. The position that you represent is only one way of achieving that end. Now, you see it as the best way to achieve the desired end state, but that doesn't make it the only way.

When did critical become a bad word? If we aren't critical of each other—words, ideas, actions—we can never get better. Critical is meant to build up, to make better. We misuse critical when we use it to break someone down. The culture of "don't @ me" is a culture of fear. We don't want the identity threat of the critical debate because we don't trust the critical parties.

Stop striving for happiness in your interactions. **Happiness is not a measure of success in your outcomes.**

Mindset. Mindset. Mindset. It's all about mindset.

Negotiation is not an individual endeavor. In fact, I'm going to argue that we live in a world in which nothing we do and nothing we achieve is done or achieved individually.

Salespeople are notoriously suspicious of the joint gain ideas that I teach. The feeling is usually that their experience overrides the need for what they perceive to be tricks. And much like religious converts, the skeptics who do convert from their sales view to the joint gain view of the world are always the best evangelists.

I have a former student who is in medical equipment sales. We recently had lunch and a pretty deep discussion about negotiation. He shares my belief that human interaction is, at its essence, a negotiation. He took my class almost ten years ago and has put the ideas to the test. He sells a variety of medical equipment, from what he termed "disposables" up to capital equipment. The disposables are items that are only used once, either because they are left in the human body (such as a stent) or because they can only be used once, such as needles. These items take a very specific strategy to sell. Since these products are commodities, there is not much difference between his products and his competitors. The negotiation doesn't really focus on the benefits of the product. The differences are negligible.

So, how can you build a joint gain in this negotiation? I get this question in class quite often. When faced with a price-only commodity negotiation, how can you build value? This is a zero-sum game, right? Either the hospital buys from my student or they buy from his competitor.

However, that's a false constraint. My student took the ideas presented and asked himself—from the customer's perspective, where is the value? The person making a buying decision is the

chapter 5

JOINT GAIN

CFO, not the doctor, so there is no preference for the commodity. Rather, what the buyer has in this interaction is a preference for the seller. It comes down to a price *and* relationship question in the negotiation.

Let's get a little deeper. To understand it better, he couldn't uncouple the capital equipment negotiations with the same CFO. Like many corporations, this hospital had many people in the room for the capital expenditure negotiations. My student knew that the CFO was the ultimate decision-maker. So, after presentations and discussions, he asked for a one-on-one meeting with her. Everyone else cleared out of the conference room and my student very genuinely asked her, "What do you need in this negotiation to be successful with your constituents?" That is a pretty jarring question for most people in a negotiation. It is essentially, how do you win? That put the CFO on the defensive because there was a definite chance my student was trying to use a dirty trick to get an advantage. That's what we often think when something seems too good to be true.

My student didn't have a long-term relationship with the CFO at this time, so there was no built-in trust. The CFO asked why she should trust him—and this is a very important key for those of us trying to get better in negotiation—he had a believable answer. He said, "If I treat you wrong, I'll never do business in this hospital, and maybe the system, again. If I do get a small one-time gain from you, it will be short lived." That was enough to convince her to give him a shot and he delivered. She looked great to the executive management and my student got a gain and looked good to his management.

This started a long-term relationship with a consistent message that ran through it. My student looked for ways to deliver benefits that were positive for the CFO. He built a level of trust so deep that when a new product was released and held to a different pricing standard, he was able to go to the CFO and say, "You've gained a lot in the past, and you're going to gain a lot in the future, but on this deal, I need you to pay the higher price." And she did it!

This is the essence of joint gain!

I don't think that I am going to get the biggest gain every time I negotiate. The other parties should think they are going to get the biggest gain. We must look for ways to benefit each other. We have to look for the ways that, together, everyone does better. If we run this scenario through the competitive idea of negotiation, it never happens. If you sit with the CFO and get her to give you a shot, and you try to maximize your own positional gain, the negotiation becomes competitive, drops back to zero-sum, and ends quickly. But, if both sides continuously build value for each other, then when faced with an issue, there is trust. Trust makes it possible to build value in adversity.

Now, back to the commodity. My student had a long-term, trusting, value-creating relationship. He wanted to get into the commodity aspect of the business as well as the capital equipment business. He asked the CFO about the business, and she replied that his competitor had that business. Most of the time, in that situation, we would leverage the relationship, drop the price, or use some other tactic to try and fight for business.

My student did none of those things.

He thanked her for the information and honored her decision. Then he left. But he didn't forget. He thought about it quite a bit. He knew that the CFO had done business with his competitor for years in the specific commodity he was trying to break into. He knew the competitor's pricing was slightly less. And he knew the way the budget worked. There was a line item for the commodity, not a price per piece.

So, the next negotiation with the CFO included a question about the commodity again. However, my student had thought pretty deeply about the CFO's perspective since the last meeting. He asked her about her relationship with the competitor—"...Must be a good relationship, since you've done business so long..." She said it was. This was great information and the last piece of information he needed.

"You have a good relationship with my competitor, and they are a great company. You have a great relationship with me, too, and our product is highly regarded in the industry. I know you want to keep a good relationship with my competitor, and you won't stop buying from them. But can you benefit me also? Could you buy one of my products for each two of the competitor products you buy?" or each three? Or four?

The CFO's perspective is to keep the relationship with both companies. My student wants any gain he can get. Selling one for each two or three or four is more than he is selling now. It increases the gain. If he doesn't ask, it won't happen.

This only works after a relationship of trust is built up. It worked with the CFO because my student was transparent about his goals and interests and dynamic in fulfilling those interests.

You can't get something if you don't ask for it. You can't ask for something if you haven't built the trust that you need. You can't build trust unless you are transparent with your interests.

When we left the lunch, my student took a to-go bag with him. A cardiologist had asked him to bring a sandwich back for him. Always building the relationship and the trust, my student obviously obliged. This is not a novel idea—buying lunch for someone who can champion you and your business—but the way you do it is pretty important. You have probably done something like this, but was it obvious that you did it to receive something back? The idea of reciprocation is powerful. But you have to do it with the right spirit. Robert Cialdini puts it great in his book *Influence:* "Don't tell them 'No problem, it was nothing.' But rather, tell them, 'I'm glad to give you this benefit because I know that you'd do the same for me.'"

> *"By an act of faith, Abel brought a better sacrifice to God than Cain. It was what he believed, not what he brought, that made the difference. That's what God noticed and approved as righteous"* (Heb 11:4 The Message).

Motive means everything.

In the joint gain view of negotiation, the motive that you bring to the negotiation is very important. Reciprocity is important, but we all know that friends or family members will help us, but only because they want something in return. Maybe we have been that person. Or, maybe we see that motive more in our work life than in our family life. When our boss asks us to do something, do we think about how we can leverage that for our own gain? How about a peer? A subordinate?

I see it a lot in the university setting. Faculty serve on committees not out of duty or because it's the right thing to do for the greater good but to gain an advantage over others. I am not saying that it's improper to gain an advantage through your service and actions. In fact, that's not only acceptable but recommended. What I am saying is that the motive you take into the interaction is critical.

Are you doing the committee work solely because you can use it to leverage a favor or an advantage later? Or are you doing it because there is an expectation, a requirement, or a need? Are you doing it out of a genuine desire to contribute? Substitute whatever it is that you do at your job, in your circle of friends, at your church, or in your family.

I can think of many instances when I see this. The student who sends me an email before the semester begins, "Dear Dr. Meyer, I heard that your class is the most amazing class in the history of learning. I'm currently number 7 on the waitlist, and I need this class to graduate this semester. Is there anything you can do to give me a seat...?" Well, it's not always that awkward, but you get the point. We can tell when a compliment isn't sincere when the motive is selfish.

What we are looking for is some empathy.

When you talk to the customer service representative, don't give them the over-the-top, insincere compliment. Give them true empathy. "How is your day going? I imagine you have to talk to a lot of disappointed customers. Does it take a toll on you? It would take a toll on me." Motive is everything. Make it a sincere conversation.

"If you've gotten anything at all out of following Christ, if his

love has made any difference in your life, if being in a community of the Spirit means anything to you, if you have a heart, if you care—then do me a favor: Agree with each other, love each other, be deep-spirited friends. Don't push your way to the front; don't sweet-talk your way to the top. Put yourself aside, and help others get ahead. Don't be obsessed with getting your own advantage. Forget yourselves long enough to lend a helping hand" (Ph 2:1-4 The Message).

"Do everything readily and cheerfully—no bickering, no second-guessing allowed! Go out into the world uncorrupted, a breath of fresh air in this squalid and polluted society. Provide people with a glimpse of good living and of the living God. Carry the light-giving Message into the night so I'll have good cause to be proud of you on the day that Christ returns" (Ph 2:14-16 The Message).

People can tell the difference between a self-focused motive and a motive that takes others into account. It has an impact on someone's desire to work with you but also on the desire to honor the deal and continue to work together.

Your motive should be for the maximum joint gain possible.

This doesn't mean you should be motivated to benefit the other party and not yourself, just as you should not be motivated to benefit only yourself. The focus should be on using interdependence in the relationship to benefit everyone involved as much as possible. Isn't that the type of negotiator with whom you want to interact? Wouldn't you rather do business with someone who is going to work hard to make sure all the value of the interaction gets realized?

Not surprising—this is a book that approaches negotiation from a Christian perspective—but is it a realistic assertion?

The thesis of this book, my classes, the training I do, and every time I talk about negotiation is this: it's not that you can negotiate in this way and gain; it's that you *should* because science supports that this is the best way to negotiate.

That's right. The question I proposed at the beginning of the book, "How can I maintain my Christian values and still be a successful negotiator?" is answered with, to get the most, you must. You need to strongly advocate for your interests and for your outcomes. You also need to be willing to consider the others involved. You need to advocate for their outcomes just as strongly as you advocate for your own. Stop trying to win. Start trying to be the best business partner for your customers, suppliers, and employees.

If you are the best partner, it's unlikely others will exploit you, as that will end a lucrative relationship for them. To be a desireable negotiation partner you should focus on three categories that cross the boundaries of secular and spiritual concerns: concern for others, the munificence of creation (the world), and stewardship of resources.

Now for the science behind it. There is no shortage of studies that examine competitive processes in negotiation. Most of these studies assume a one-sided transaction; that is, they look at the negotiation from a specific point of view. The question asked is often, *Will the buyer, seller, or specific side in the negotiation achieve the outcome that they desire?* Recently this has changed.

The focus is now more on the entirety of the outcome. Did the interdependence result in an increase in resources? That's the question we should be asking. Whether one party or another had an increase is nice, but the reason we work together is that the interdependence results in an overall increase. We get more together than we could apart.

This was tested in a study that looked at the motive one brings to a negotiation, combined with the behavior used in the negotiation.

Make no mistake, science is nice but not necessary for a Christian in the world. We are called to follow God's desire for our lives, and not just when science supports it. It so happens that, in this case, God's commands and the science behind negotiation are aligned. This is the beauty of our Creator once again reflected in the natural order of life. We see this often in nature. It's not as obvious in an organizational setting.

The organization is something that man has leveraged for his own use, to produce, to control, to remove ambiguity in life. But God's sovereignty shows through.

Here is some of the science behind the joint-gain idea of negotiation. I will return to this science as I further develop these ideas in the book.

Concern For Others

It's obvious to most that God has called us to be concerned about the welfare of others. He tells us to love our neighbors as we love ourselves, to care for widows and orphans, and through the Apostle Paul, he instructed the early church to organize and pool their resources so that everyone could live well.

That's great for the church, but we're talking about business. Yes, your company does a charity drive at the end of the year. You give to Toys for Tots. You recycle. You have a mission statement that says to put customers first. All of that is good. But when you are sitting one-on-one with a supplier, what drives that interaction? What about when you are dealing with a difficult customer? Or when you have to work in a team setting with a peer that is known to be a free rider—that one person who won't do anything to further the team goals but will take a lot of credit when the project is complete?

How do you show concern in your daily interactions? How should you?

What typically happens is a focus on self. We first make sure that our own outcomes are safe, and after that, we may move to take care of others.

Be careful in reading this next part. I am not suggesting that you should be concerned with only the outcomes of others. I am not saying that you should ignore your own outcomes or not concern yourself with your goals. That would be foolish. I'm not even saying that you should put your goals and interests second.

What I want you to understand is the power of motive. When your motive is to compete, everyone gets less. When your motive is toward a collaborative, joint gain ideal, everyone gets more. Some research done by Laurie Weingart from Carnegie Mellon University looks at the motives people brought into a complex multiparty negotiation. She found that those who were motivated for joint gain were concerned that everyone in the negotiation got their interests met and produced more overall gains for all parties in the negotiation. But the interesting part is that they produced more, and everyone got more, even when they used competitive tactics. So, the motive that they took into the negotiation was more important than the tactics they used during the negotiation.

Another way to state it: What you think before you enter the negotiation is more important than what you do while you are negotiating. If you think about beating the other party, you won't do as well as if you think about making gains for everyone involved.

The other important takeaway from this study is that the joint-gain-motivated negotiators also got more themselves. They wanted to be sure that everyone got more and that led to them getting more. If you bring resources to the table, if you are the provider, you can ask for more of the eventual outcome for yourself. Being the negotiator who seeks to benefit others opens the door for you to benefit yourself.

And you can ask boldly.

The Munificence of God's Creation

Negotiators adopt one of two mindsets about the availability of resources in the negotiation. Munificence says that there is an extravagance of resources available if you are creative about looking. Scarcity takes the opposite view and says that resources are limited, difficult to come by, and should be fought over.

This fits right in with the idea of motive. And again, the science supports the idea of approaching the negotiation with a munificence mindset. If you come in with the idea that you have many ways to meet your interests and many outcomes that will be successful, you don't have to be positional and negative in your bargaining. If you have an idea that resources are scarce, the negotiation becomes zero-sum. Every dollar, every gain, every resource that goes to others in the negotiation comes out of your pocket.

This makes negotiators very positional. They end up going into a negotiation with a singular successful outcome in their head and they fight for it instead of being open to other possible ways to achieve their interest.

Stewardship of Resources

Why do we miss this as a society? Amoral leadership plays a big role. It's not something that is talked about much, so let's start that conversation.

Amoral leadership isn't immoral leadership. Amoral leadership is when leaders are silent on the idea of right and wrong. It means that your manager never makes a judgment publicly about whether a decision is right or wrong. It's the accepted way that we interact in society today. It's the classic "you do you" response. However, not taking a stand about what is right or wrong leads people to make decisions that are immoral. Negotiators are no longer burdened with an organization that demands the right response and can make different decisions about how people are treated. I'm not saying that organizations are actively supporting employee actions that are harmful to others; rather, I am saying that organizations are not demanding that employees do the right thing for others to benefit them.

Negotiation is more than just a business activity. Whenever people can work together to gain together, that's a negotiation. So, we want to be deliberate in our negotiations. We want to include every interaction: when we go to the grocery store, when we sit at home with our family, when we pass our boss in the hallway. All of these interactions are important and impact our outcomes.

In the context of power, one question that I get quite often when I'm talking to folks about negotiation is: How do I get the upper hand in this negotiation? How can I leverage my resources or information to get the upper hand? It's a common question.

I think we grossly overestimate what the upper hand means in negotiation. We take the upper hand and depend on it, which can give us a sense of entitlement in our negotiations.

What does the upper hand mean?

I had a discussion not too long ago with a gentleman who was putting together a video about using power in negotiations. There are many misconceptions about what power looks like in negotiations, and one of his questions was, *When we're involved with a powerful negotiator, how should we try to undermine that power?* That's the default behavior. When we see someone who has more power, we try to take that power, or decrease that power. People think about it as a way to shift the power dynamic when there's asymmetrical power, when one party is much more powerful than the other.

How do we deal with situations where there's asymmetrical power?

A very common thought is to undermine or look for a way to reduce that power. What does undermining somebody's power mean? Think about the rhetoric behind it, about how our words and language reflect our attitudes. Our behavior reveals our motives.

So, if we're saying, "I'm trying to undermine somebody's power," we are essentially trying to destroy their power by some nefarious means. That is going to impact our mindset and follow us into the interaction. That behavior is added to our negotiating reputation. We become known as a negotiator that destroys others. It's rarely that overt, but we all know that person in our organization who is difficult or demanding or hard to work with, or the person who's just known to be a jerk. Those are the people who work through fear, who undermine power, who make others around them *less* rather than bringing more to the table. Those are the people who make negotiation a difficult task—the ones who always want the upper hand. Those negotiators who bring power to the interaction also bring resources. If we want to get more, undermining that should be the last thing we do.

Most negotiations are not high stakes. They are run-of-the-mill, day-to-day interactions. Sure, they can be high-dollar. Yes, you could lose your job, but you won't lose your life. You could lose your integrity, your moral grounding, and that will cost you more than losing the deal.

I'm not willing to compromise my values for a short-term gain in an interaction. I'm not willing to harm another for my own gain. I think that if asked, most people would agree with that statement. I also think, in practice, people hurt others routinely and write it off as "Just business."

We need to be more deliberate and demanding with our settlements. If we are unwilling to accept a bad deal for ourselves, why not be unwilling to accept a bad deal for others involved in the negotiation?

Be more demanding. Use phrases like, "I think we can do better." "I want everyone to leave with a good outcome." "Does this deal work for you?" These phrases show that we care about the others involved, and in turn, they will care more about us.

We need to be aware that there is an insidious bias toward settlement in negotiation. This is a well-documented and studied scientific phenomenon. We put so much work into our negotiations that we are unwilling to walk away without a settlement. This wouldn't be a big deal, but many negotiators use it to their advantage. Knowing that people don't want to leave without a deal and using it against them are two very different ideas.

I'm not sure that negotiators enter the interaction with the idea that they will put people in the desperate situation of accepting a bad deal or walking away without a deal, but it happens a lot. When I bring this up in training sessions, everyone wants to talk about buying cars. It's true some car salespeople use this tactic—but they aren't the only ones.

When you buy a car, they do a lot of things to get you invested in the deal. The test drive makes you identify with the car emotionally. The length of the process, the number of people that you have to go through, the paperwork, all of this is meant to produce a commitment to the process. You think, "I can't walk away; I have so much invested at this point." You may not think it explicitly, but it's a psychological phenomenon called escalation of commitment. It's when you proceed with a course of action beyond what is rational.

You've been at the dealership all day. You've worked on the paperwork. You've run the numbers. You think about starting the process over if you don't buy the car—and you think about how much you loved it during the test drive.

And the salesperson knows this.

When I was buying a car for my daughter, we went through the process. We got close to the end, but she was thorough. There was another car that she was interested in at a different dealership. I didn't think it was the right car for her, but she wanted to look. Since we weren't ready to do the deal I told the salesperson, "We need to look at one other car, but I think this is the deal for us." He had that look of defeat on his face. I told him we would be back the next weekend.

When we walked in the next weekend, he should be genuinely surprised. "You came back!" I told him I did what I said. He said, "You're the only one. When people walk out, they never come back." That's the other side of the settlement bias. When negotiators fail in the negotiation, they don't come back to it. Many negotiators come to the negotiation with an all-or-nothing mindset. The settlement bias reinforces this thinking. People stay too long in a failing negotiation and then don't come back to a promising negotiation. I don't know if I would have come back if we bought the other car; I'd like to think that I would have. I would like to know if someone made a decision that impacted my life. I imagine the salesperson wanted to know as well. As I discovered, he had already made an assumption.

If we enter with a mindset that everyone is going to gain, it can address this bias. The settlement bias exists in negotiation because negotiators believe that they are in a competitive interaction for scarce resources.

We know this isn't true, either from a sacred perspective or a worldly one. Negotiations aren't inherently competitive. We make them that way out of the fear of losing.

> *"But God gave us a spirit not of fear but of power and love and self-control"* (2 Timothy 1:7).

We need to love the other party, be concerned for their outcome, and expand the outcome for all involved. That's how we would want the others in the negotiation to act toward us. Scripture is vocal on this aspect.

> *"Do nothing from selfish ambition or conceit, but in humility count others more significant than yourselves. Let each of you look not only to his own interests, but also to the interests of others. Have this mind among yourselves, which is yours in Christ Jesus"* (Philippians 2:3-5).

> *"What good is it for someone to gain the whole world, yet forfeit their soul? Or what can anyone give in exchange for their soul? If anyone is ashamed of me and my words in this adulterous and sinful generation, the Son of Man will be ashamed of them when he comes in his Father's glory with the holy angels"* (Mark 8:36-38).

You may not have read these selections in the context of negotiation. When I read scripture, I think about every interaction as a negotiation. Jesus was the best negotiator to ever walk the earth. Because he is God, he sees the munificence in every interaction. He always pushed for the greatest gain for all involved. God's economy isn't constrained. The decisions that we make as negotiators are determined by whose economy we embrace, God's or man's.

Think about the entitlement rhetoric we use to undermine people. We focus on what we deserve or what we are owed. The words we use matter. Research shows that those with entitlement attitudes in negotiation use those attitudes to destroy integrative outcomes.

Rhetoric is a big problem in our interactions. Think about how we refer to our negotiation interactions. We use a lot of competitive, zero-sum, win-lose language. "Did they get the best of you?" "Did you win?" "I'm going to beat them." "I'm going to crush that goal." We talk about the people who are involved in the interaction as adversaries. Like we are working against them. We sit on different sides of the table. We do/say/ask/show things that are meant to make them uncomfortable.

Why?

Fear.

Wait, hear me out. I'm not saying that you're scared! I'm saying we fear the ambiguity of the situation. It's part of human nature. When we are faced with ambiguity, we do whatever we can to reduce it.

Because of that fear, we assign rhetoric to the negotiation that we think will alleviate that ambiguity. We fear what will happen in the secular business world if we use different words and language. So, we embrace competitive rhetoric—the words and actions that seem to be strong.

Strong is another part of the rhetoric of negotiation. Is it strong to bully someone? Is it strong to be competitive and demanding? Is it strong to take an unrelenting attitude toward our original positions? Do you think that people want to do business with those who act this way?

I believe it's weak to take that competitive stance. It's not a strength to be unwilling to adjust or consider other possibilities. It's cowardice. Hiding behind a preconceived position, not being open to other ideas to get your interests met, that's fear of ambiguity. You hadn't thought of that outcome, and so you aren't certain how it will end for you. Fear isn't strong; it's weak.

It's also positional thinking. If you don't have a clear idea about your interests, you've only done the work far enough to have built a position that will be acceptable, but you don't know why you're in the room negotiating, you don't know what your interdependence can gain you. You aren't prepared.

You aren't prepared.

If you can't point to the gain from the interdependence, the reality is that you don't know why you are negotiating.

And for those of you in business, sales, purchasing, etc., the interest is NEVER money. Money is a position. It's an interest substitution. When we are trying to point to money, it's usually because we haven't spent enough time figuring out the gain we get from the interdependent relationship.

So, strength in negotiation isn't tough positional bargaining. It's not standing your ground, refusing to give in. Strength in negotiation is awareness of the interdependence in the relationship and understanding the gain from negotiating in the first place.

Strength is knowing not only how the relationship and the interaction benefit us but also how they benefit the others in the negotiation. Strength is bringing resources to the interaction, being open to creative solutions that are possible, and being curious and willing. But strength is also being unwilling to accept a deal that doesn't fulfill your interests. Really strong negotiators are also unwilling to accept a deal that doesn't fulfill the interests of the other parties involved.

Think of it from a family or close relationship standpoint. You show strength when you provide for the good of the group. It's not just an economic question. Strength isn't only the money you earn to provide for your family, its more. It's the safety, the freedom, the self-actualization, the love that you show.

Negotiation is the same. Better quality of relationship and being closer to love means better interactions. Think about negotiating with people you dislike and tell me that you do as well as with those you like. I negotiate with people I dislike, and I know how I should treat them in the interaction to get the best outcome. But I don't like them. I don't trust them.

Even though I know the research, I still fall prey to this type of interaction. It's human nature. The research tells us that when we feel threatened, we increase our defenses. We stick to our positions, and we won't give any concessions.

You aren't able to fix the people you don't trust. It's especially hard if it's a person in a position of power—your biggest customer, your boss, or any important person in your life. You can work on it. You can try.

But you can fix you. You can be sure that you are open and trustworthy. You can be sure that you are pushing for the most in interactions, that you are transparent about interests, and that you are willing to consider creative outcomes.

Being the most desirable negotiation partner is easier said than done. The rest of this book will focus on how you can make it happen.

Negotiation is an interactive event and depends on multiple people to achieve an outcome. Because of the interactive nature of this event, you can never completely control the outcome. You can control the priorities and values that you bring to the interaction, and you can influence the outcome through the relationships and interactions, but you can't control the outcome.

Building Relationships

I was at a meeting not long ago, sitting around the table and having a discussion with the gentleman that was sitting to my left. We know each other; we're friends. We have a casual relationship but I wouldn't say it is deep. He knows that I am a professor and he asked what I teach. As soon as I said negotiation, he wanted to tell me a story that obviously meant a lot to him. This gentleman works in the software industry. Since I also worked in the software industry, we had some things in common.

The largest customer for his software firm had an issue with a bug in the software. Because of this bug they couldn't get their mission critical work done. So, they called in this gentleman, a couple of his coworkers, and their boss, trying to get a resolution. It's always a little bit intimidating when the boss is sitting in the room for the negotiation with your largest customer.

My friend said that everybody from his

company was sitting on one side of the table and everybody from the customer's company was sitting on the other side of the table. Not an atypical way to run a meeting. During the discussion about the issue, the customer said, "We can't get our work done until we fix this problem! So, what are you going to do about it?" No one had a response for the customer, and they all sat there quietly. Then the boss stood up, picked up his chair, moved it to the other side of the table next to the customer, and said "OK, let's get to work. What are we going to do to fix the problem?"

This action had an incredible impact on my friend. His point in telling it to me was to illustrate something that we don't always understand. We view our relationships in very limited, structured ways. We assume that the important relationships in the story are defined by the organizational lines. Yes, we all agree that there is something important about the relationship with the customer but notice what the boss did in this interaction. He put the importance on the relationship with the customer—even to the point of "switching sides."

While it was a symbolic move, the symbolism carried a heavy weight. Everyone on his team understood that he was saying. *If the customer has this problem with the software, then I also have this problem with the software.*

How does that impact the relationship with the customer? The CEO stands with you in your requests of his team. That's how to put the relationship first. That's how you move someone to want to do business with you. That's how you build trust.

But what does that do to the relationship with your team if you are the CEO?

There is a fine line to walk—and a lot of the impact lies in the preceding interactions and the follow-up to this interaction. If you already have a great relationship with the team, if you already have solid trust built, this will be expected and accepted. If you have the relationship, the team will already understand your values. And then, when the interaction is over, the discussion needs to be about how we all succeed together.

This had a big impact on how my friend viewed his work relationships and how he got the job done. They were losing millions of dollars over the time that this problem was occurring. When the CEO switched to the other side of the table, it made the entire interaction less competitive and more of a partnership.

Roger Fisher, author of the book *Getting to Yes*, the precursor to modern negotiation thought, says that *taking the perspective of the other parties in a negotiation is the most critical skill.* Similarly, Stuart Diamond, author of the book *Getting More,* talks about seeing the pictures in the heads of those with whom we're negotiating. Both of these negotiation experts are pointing us to think about the issues in the interaction from the perspective of the others involved. What are they thinking? Why would they be thinking that? How would this outcome impact them?

Both of these ideas are after the same end result: to understand the others involved in the interaction. We desire to understand others so that we can build a relationship with them, so that we can understand the interdependence and how it's important.

The body language of standing up, moving a chair, and yourself, says, *I'm here so that I can get the perspective of the people who are important to me.* That's something we need to learn to do in our day-to-day negotiations. That's one of the major keys to building a relationship. We need to take the perspective of the others in the relationship and let them know that their perspective is important to us.

Some current research shows that empathy and perspective-taking are critical for problem-solving and critical thinking—two important aspects of finding the best outcome in negotiations.

This suggests that when we are taking the perspective of others, we understand that they want to benefit. They are involved in the interaction because they want to gain from it. And the others should understand that you want to get a benefit also. Often, we hear bad advice that says to hide your benefit, or worse, act like you are disappointed in the outcome, that you didn't get what you really wanted. This, of course, is in the spirit of trying to get as much as you can from others in the interaction.

But imagine how that would make someone feel. Do you want to leave people in a bad place after your interaction? If you do, you are missing the point of this book. Hopefully, you want to be a desirable negotiation partner. Hopefully, you want to benefit others while also getting the maximum benefit possible for yourself.

If we leave feeling that the others didn't achieve their objective, it can impact the relationship. If the truth comes out that it was a good outcome, that impacts trust. It's much better if everyone involved knows that interests were met.

If I am a perspective taker, I can be happy for your positive outcome because that's what I want, too. In fact, if I'm good at taking other's perspectives, I should want you to get your most important interests met. I won't let you settle for less than maximizing your interests because I wouldn't settle for less.

As a Christian, I base my relationships and interactions on the ideas from 1 Corinthians 12:27, which tells me we are all linked; we are all connected. We are part of one body, and Jesus Christ is the head of that body. In the body, the hands don't compete against the feet. The lungs don't compete with the fingers. If your body doesn't work together in collaborative harmony, you can't get to the outcomes you need to achieve. Much the same, we need to be collaborative with our partners in business. If we are in competition, we can't achieve the best results.

There are times when we put in proxies for trust or build contingencies rather than taking the time or effort to build trust. There's nothing wrong with contingencies, but for important relationships or interactions, I don't want those contingencies to replace trust. I want to build trust because trust facilitates easier interactions and greater outcomes.

That means I'm going to be the one that brings some value to our interaction. I will give you the information that you desire because that shows I'm trustworthy; and that the relationship is important to me. I'm not going to give away the farm. I'm not going to tell you things I shouldn't. I'm not going to tell you things you can leverage against me in a negotiation, but I am going to give you valuable information centered around my interests. I'm going to paint the picture and make sure you know how I gain from our interdependence.

I am not going to make you guess. I am going to make my perspective really easy for you. In return, I'm going to ask you to paint your picture for me. I will ask you to tell me what's important to you. That's going to build the relationship.

The next thing we must consider is our own moral and ethical ideas about how to build the relationship. The book of Romans, chapter 12, says we want to love what is good and contribute to the needs of others. When people persecute you, instead of cursing them back, bless them.

You are going to negotiate with difficult people. You can approach it defensively and competitively. You can return negative emotions and behavior. That's going to produce a relationship that's tense. Or you can return positivity and even love and see how that changes your relationship with the difficult negotiator.

In Matthew 6, Jesus tells us that we should not worry about earthly things. But this is how we spend most of our relational capital, trying to get things. Jesus says to seek first the kingdom of God, and the rest will work itself out. He's not saying we will get everything we want. He's saying we don't always need the things we want, and we rarely focus on the things that are important. Let's apply this to your interactions. Do you have people in your life you just want to benefit from without a thought of getting something out of it? When you interact with your spouse, significant other, or children, do you keep a scorecard? Do you think about who got the benefit last and try to even things up?

Of course, we don't. We value the relationship because it is important to us and because we trust that the others involved in the relationship value it similarly.

It's not just scripture that leads us down this path. The research corroborates this idea. We talked about the research from Kern, Brett, and Weingart that shows those who enter a relationship motivated to search for overall benefit, that is, benefits for all those involved, do better than negotiators who are focused on their own gain. If you value the others involved, it pays off.

Lying

It's not uncommon when I'm talking to people about my research or training in negotiation that eventually we turn to the topic of lying. Very often, people are sheepish about bringing it up because we are tempted, or we do lie about our positions in negotiation. It's a very common thing. There are some studies from 1999 and 2005 reported in a recent Harvard Business Review article that look at the amount of lying in negotiation. These studies show that over 50% of people admit to lying in a negotiation.

Think about that for a minute: over 50% admit to lying. How many are not admitting to it? If you are lying in your negotiation, you probably aren't proud of it. You probably want to hide it. So, if 50% of people are saying, "Yes, I lie during a negotiation occasionally"—and remember, lying can be lies of omission, it can be shading the truth, it can be hiding some fact from somebody, or actively seeking to obfuscate the facts—if 50% of people are willing to admit that, how many more are not admitting they lie?

This is an issue that we desperately need to address. The question is, should I lie in my negotiations? Should I shade the truth? Should I hide some facts from people if they're going to lie to me? If they're going to hide facts from me, shouldn't I protect myself and do the same?

This is how we approach many of our interactions. If you treat me one way, I'll treat you the same in return. Remember the tit-for-tat strategy discussed earlier? Axelrod found clear evidence that this was a common response for people. It's a very simple strategy, but widely used. He said that people enter an interaction with the desire to cooperate but will repay the same behavior that others show to them.

Follow this through to its logical conclusion. If I am that desirable negotiation partner and I enter the negotiation with an intention to work cooperatively to maximize gain, but you are a competitive negotiator, then, given the information from Axelrod, I will be acting as a competitive negotiator quickly. Even if I move first in a collaborative way, the other negotiator will respond in a competitive way, which will lead me to respond in kind. This will elicit another competitive move from the other negotiator, and now we are in a spiral of competitive, zero-sum negotiation. And we can't get out.

But, if I enter the negotiation with my interest firmly in place, and I understand that the interdependence of the interaction is critical to achieve my goals, and I'm willing to persevere in my collaborative strategy, eventually the other negotiators will see that they could change the interaction and the outcome for the better.

It's not an easy task. This is where the collaborative negotiator proves their strength. You need to persist in the collaborative strategies in the face of competitive others. Research tells us that over 80% of negotiators will abandon collaborative negotiating within five minutes when negotiating with a competitive negotiator. It's the tit-for-tat mentality.

But if you persist, you can change the interaction.

Why should you persist?

The scriptural answer is that we are all part of each other through the body of Christ (1 Cor 12:27), and therefore, we should be just as concerned for others as we are for ourselves. I know that should be enough, but we live in a world where people are concerned about their jobs, about mouths to feed, about paying for internet access and smartphones. This can get in the way sometimes.

Besides the benefits of the Christ-like response to the interaction, let's talk about the evidence that we have from research.

The most common fear I run across regarding collaborative methods for negotiation is that the collaborative negotiator asks the other side what they want out of the interaction, and they end up giving away a lot of value while receiving little in return. That's not collaboration, that's acquiescence. Those are different strategies.

When my wife asks me for something, I adopt the strategy of acquiescence (mostly, I hope, maybe don't check up on me…). When my boss asks me for something, if I adopt an attitude of acquiescence I will soon be overwhelmed at work. It will feel as if I'm in a one-sided relationship and that she is taking advantage of me. We don't want others to take advantage of us; this is why we are reticent to adopt a collaborative mindset.

This is how I want you to think about the collaborative mindset. When you enter the negotiation, enter with a motive to collaborate and create value. While you are involved in the negotiation, be mindful of what and how you are giving. Don't give unconditionally. Don't create value and reap none of the rewards. Create value and use it to trade for value that is important to you. The research tells us that entering the negotiation with a competitive mindset is what leads us to be positional, to hide information, or to lie. The competitive mindset leads us down the zero-sum competitive path.

However, if we enter the negotiation with a collaborative mindset—the desire to create joint-gains for all those involved (including ourselves!)—we will head down a different path. That path leads to more value creation. It leads to greater outcomes. It leads to better intangible outcomes, such as better relationships, better feelings about the outcome, and better feelings about the process.

But only if we persist!

Again, you should not lie in your negotiations. There are two reasons you should not lie. The first is the ethical and moral aspect. The second is a research-based reason. The Christian moral and ethical view says that lying is morally wrong. It's not the way that we want to do business. It's damaging to our relationships.

But in the business world, people lie or hide information or allow you to believe something that's untrue. In the business world, you need to work with these people who are going to apply the same moral and ethical fabric as me differently—people who are going to view lying as a part of business or taking advantage of others as a part of doing business.

I've heard the "it's just business" phrase used to excuse a lot of questionable behavior. But I want you to consider this: how would you feel if your spouse or significant other used that to excuse some terrible behavior? What that phrase means is that the behavior is ok because it was in pursuit of an organizational goal.

When it comes to the research-based reason, when you lie, you send people down the wrong path to achieve the goal. If I lie to you about what's important in the negotiation relationship and you are motivated to get an outcome that meets my needs, you rely on inaccurate information to achieve those outcomes—it doesn't move me in the right direction. When there are lies in the negotiation, it shrinks the potential bargaining zone. There are roadblocks between your desired outcome and the positions that are being presented based on the lies.

And when the lie is contradicted, we lose trust. If we make a statement in the negotiation that is a misdirection, falsehood, or a blatant lie, trust is broken. I see this a lot with people who are trying to bully others into a specific position, particularly a monetary position. Maybe you've heard this before. "That's as low as I can go; I can't go any lower, or I will be selling at a loss." But then as you start to walk away the negotiator makes a lower offer to keep you there. Maybe you have said or done this in your negotiations. The ultimatum.

You may think you are winning but, believe me, you aren't. First, you are eroding trust. This is one of the reasons that people dislike or even fear negotiations. They feel that everyone is trying to take advantage of them. It's an overstatement, but when you see people behaving this way, it's easy to see why some would think others are trying to take advantage of them.

It's a problem that has been around for a long time. The prophet Jeremiah in the twelfth verse of his book says, "Why does the way of the wicked prosper? Why do the faithless live at ease?" We don't like feeling like a situation is unjust.

And the reality of the situation is that WE DON'T KNOW if the other party is lying. We don't know if the other party did better than we did. We often don't know if we achieved our own goal in the negotiation. If we don't have a solid benchmark, we won't know if we have done well in the interaction. What we often do is look at the difference between our first offer—which was the big aggressive ask—and what we ended up with—which is the much more reasonable outcome, and we are disappointed. There is very often a lot of space between the first offer and the final outcome because we have had to give up value with concessions, so it feels like a loss. Our experience is based on the relationship and trust in the interaction, and questions about the veracity of the truth erode that trust.

There is another issue at work here, the term fairness. I don't like to use the term fairness in negotiations because it is subjective. What I see as fair, you may see as unfair. However, we have a term in organizational science for the perceptions of fairness in our interactions. We call it organizational justice. There are different types of organizational justice, and these predict somewhat different outcomes. One of these types of organizational justice is informational justice. Do others perceive that information has been shared with them in a manner that is consistent and truthful?

This perception has a lot to do with whether we build trust and the value that we put on the relationship. If I have built a relationship on something false—even something small—how can I expect trust? Would you trust someone who actively tries to give you false information or tries to hide information? It just doesn't work.

"A man reaps what he sows. Whoever sows to please their flesh, from the flesh will reap destruction; whoever sows to please the

Spirit, from the Spirit will reap eternal life. Let us not become weary in doing good, for at the proper time we will reap a harvest if we do not give up. Therefore, as we have opportunity, let us do good to all people, especially to those who belong to the family of believers" (Galatians 6: 7-10).

"Do nothing out of selfish ambition or vain conceit. Rather, in humility value others above yourselves, not looking to your own interests but each of you to the interests of the others. In your relationships with one another, have the same mindset as Christ Jesus" (Philippians 2: 3-5).

Negotiating with someone with whom we have a relationship gives us some benefits. If we have a positive or good relationship, we are more willing to ask about interests, more willing to persist in the interaction when faced with obstacles; we won't bail for our alternative at the first sign of trouble. We are more likely to look at the negotiation as a creative problem-solving exercise. We will work together with the others involved and build a creative solution to benefit as many participants as possible.

Joint gain ideas benefit greatly from a relationship.

But, there are some caveats. In a close relationship, we are more likely to assume things about our negotiation partners. We assume we know the interests of our partners, especially when it is a close and long-standing relationship. The previous interactions give us information that we use when making decisions about how to interact. If it's a close relationship, people have a tendency to overestimate the knowledge they have about the other's interests.

When we deal with those in a close relationship, we make assumptions, first about their interests and then about positions and concessions to achieve those interests. These assumptions go both ways. That means there are more likely to be some missed opportunities.

breaking

down

JOINT GAIN

Hopefully by now you're convinced that there is a better way to negotiate. I hope you're beyond thinking about beating the other party or winning the negotiation. I hope that you are beyond thinking about not losing.

If you are competing, you aren't negotiating.

It's that simple. Competing, fighting for limited resources—that's not what negotiation is about. Great negotiators know that negotiation is about expanding the potential of the interaction. The best negotiators know that focusing on the joint outcome leads to the most gain.

Negotiating is about building better outcomes for everyone.

If you are open to a new way of thinking about the negotiation process you also need to be open to some new definitions of important constructs. The foundational construct in joint-gain negotiation is the idea of interests. I don't mean if you are interested in the outcome or the relationship. An interest is a very specific idea in negotiation. It has a specific definition and it is foundational for success.

I know the term interest has a meaning that we all associate with it. Something that we are interested in is something that we would like to have or see or in which we want to participate. For instance, I'm interested in seeing that movie, I'm interested in that promotion, I'm interested in buying that house.

But I want you to think about interest in a

INTERESTS VS. POSITIONS

chapter 7

different way. I want you to think about the interest in the negotiation as the answer to the question, Why are you in the room? You need to shift your focus from the things you want to why you want those things.

Let that sink in.

You need to shift your focus from the eight percent raise you are trying to achieve to why you want that raise. Are you trying to get recognition? Are you trying to change your standard of living? Are you really trying to get a promotion but you see the raise as a necessary step? By thinking about the why instead of the what you are able to accept something other than the eight percent raise as a success. It opens you to more possibilities for success. If your focus remains on the raise and you negotiate a lower raise than you ask for—the typical split-the-difference outcome—you, your boss, and the organization have all lost as it doesn't maximize value for everyone involved.

In this example, the raise is the position. Recognition for the work is the interest. As the employee, you worked hard on a project or on the goals for the year, and you want that work to be recognized. We often have a limited view of ways in which our interests can be met, not because we've done anything wrong but because everyone approaches a negotiation with limited and biased information. Based on that limited information, you ask for a raise as the way to get your contribution recognized. But you may not have information about the company's ability to pay that raise. Or there may be other constraints that are unknown—the company is going through a restructuring, there is an IPO on the horizon, or other possibilities.

If you are focused only on the raise outcome, you may fail in your negotiation. But focus on the interest and you are open to something you've never even thought possible, like a new position created for you to best use your skills. Positional bargaining is the norm in most situations, but it doesn't have to be business as usual.

You need to have a strategy in place to get better outcomes. You can have better experiences, build more trust, and have better relationships if you start with a specific and coherent strategy. These various strategic aspects and the interplay between them will give you a leg up when you go into a negotiation. When I say leg up, I don't mean that you're going to win, because I don't view negotiation as something to win or lose.

In sports there's a winner and a loser; one team walks away disappointed with the outcome. That's not what we want with our negotiations. We want our negotiations to be positive for those involved because we want to negotiate with these people again. It's easier to negotiate a second time around, and it's easier to negotiate when you've got a solid relationship built on trust.

If you think about how to build a relationship, how to build it into a positive experience for the people you are negotiating with, it takes on a lot more strategic preparation. This might be a little bit more difficult than a purely one-sided preparation where you focus only on your own ideas and information.

This is not a one-size-fits-all way to look at your interactions. This is about your motive. More than that, this is about truly understanding your motive. And even more than that, this is about understanding the application of that motive to the interaction.

The good negotiator can use positional bargaining and end with a (mostly) successful negotiation. A great negotiator will remember the actual reason for the negotiation and will be more flexible with concessions and will end with a better outcome.

I want you to be better than a great negotiator. I want you to be the best negotiator. The best negotiators will plan before the negotiation with a focus on the underlying reason for negotiating. They will use that underlying reason to build their positions, determine their concessions, and anticipate their outcomes.

I know this is an abstract idea. Let me try to fill in some of the blanks for you with an example. Recently a student in a Master's degree program took my class. He, like many others during the pandemic, decided to move. He lived in California, close to his job. The company moved most of their employees to a work from home situation, so he and his family decided to maximize the opportunity to move from a higher cost of living state to a state that allowed for a higher standard of living: Texas. This has been a common occurrence in the past several years, one that dramatically impacted the market for real estate. Prices soared. Buyers were put in a position of low power. Sellers, it seemed, could ask for any price, and buyers were forced to pay over the asking price or risk losing the house.

Due to the volatility of the market and the uncertainty of the move, this turned into multiple different negotiations. The first sale of the student's home in California fell through, causing him to cancel the subsequent purchase of a home in Texas. Disappointment doesn't capture the depth of the emotional toll this took on both my student and his wife.

When asked about a deal like this, most people will talk about the reason for doing the deal in similar terms used by this student: maximize the exchange of dollars. Most will focus on getting the most dollars from their existing house while paying the least dollars for their new house. These are the positions (there are other positions in the negotiation—occupancy date, down payment, and the like. But to simplify this explanation, let's focus on the biggest positions).

If I am focused on the dollars in this interaction, I lose the ability to be flexible. I turn this integrative negotiation into a very distributive, zero-sum situation. I fight and claw for every single dollar. It could lead to an impasse and negatively impact my reputation. It could lead to a substandard deal. This is the real danger. When negotiators focus on the positions in their deals, they end up making compromises. You're probably thinking, "Great! Compromise is what makes negotiation possible." I'm here to tell you that compromise is a lose-lose strategy. Each party is partially satisfied.

This student explained in pretty good detail why the positional bargaining strategy would have failed. He was focused on completing their move before the end of summer because he needed to get his elementary-aged kids enrolled before the start of the school year. It was critical to him and to his wife that the kids didn't move during the school year. It's a big enough disruption to move from California to Texas. It's hard to make friends; it's hard to adjust to new routines, to new schools, new everything. My student and his wife wanted to minimize that stress. The move had to be completed before summer.

The real estate market was difficult, to say the least. If this student decided to get into an aggressive positional battle either with the seller he's working with or with the next seller, he would put himself in a position that is designed to work against both parties. Those positional battles focus only on that singular aspect that one party puts at the forefront of the interaction, typically the price.

The research tells us that it's a very common problem that is faced in negotiations. Individuals focus on a singular issue and miss the opportunity to increase the outcome with other issues. This focus often leads negotiators to completely miss that other issues exist.

Fortunately, my student had embraced the concept in class of focusing on the interest in the negotiation, rather than on the positions. This allowed him to expand the potential outcomes and not get caught in the zero-sum trap. A focus on interest allowed him to understand that moving was about more than the positional bargaining focused-on price. After the failed closing on the first house, he expanded his criteria and his available issues in the negotiation.

It's something we rarely think about doing, but it can change the way we get business done. Now, a house purchase is probably a bad example because it's not an ongoing relationship, but it still can be a collaborative endeavor. The issue that leads us to positional, zero-sum behavior is that we only see the situation from our own perspective. Or, if we see the other perspective, but we don't embrace its importance.

There are several good reasons to value the perspectives and the interests of the other parties involved in the negotiation. From a biblical perspective, we are called to value others. Most of the population can quote the Golden Rule, even if they aren't aware that it comes from Matthew 7:12.

"So, in everything, do to others what you would have them do to you, for this sums up the Law and the Prophets."

This is also stated in Luke 6:31. Paul gets more specific to the ideas at hand with his statement to the Phillippians in chapter 2:2-4.

"Then make my joy complete by being like-minded, having the same love, being one in spirit and of one mind. Do nothing out of selfish ambition or vain conceit. Rather, in humility value others above yourselves, not looking to your own interests but each of you to the interests of the others."

That is some pretty clear direction that we should be thinking past our own outcome.

From an academic standpoint, Roger Fisher was the first to declare that the ability to take the perspective of other parties in a negotiation was a determinant of better outcomes. Roger said this in 1988 in his seminal book, *Getting to Yes*. It may sound like common sense now, but the reality is that at that time, everyone was negotiating from a positional stance. They were concerned only with the outcome achieved, not the way it was achieved. This was during the timeframe of the movie *Wall Street*, and while you may not know Gordon Gekko, you likely know his catchphrase, "Greed is good." Roger's idea went against the cultural zeitgeist of the time. He went against all the people who were reading *The Art of War* and trying to destroy and dominate in the business world.

It didn't really take hold.

To some extent, people were less open about their desire to dominate. I worked in the world of commission-based sales. I wouldn't say that we had the needs and desires of others as a focus. Have you tried to buy a car lately? How did that go? Did you walk away saying, "Wow, what a great experience!" or were you frustrated by the talk of the supply chain and chip shortage?

The same can be said for the housing market in recent years. My student had a deal fall through, and that caused him to re-evaluate the situation. When he found the next house, he talked to the buyers through his agent. He made sure that the buyers knew he was interested in the house because he had young kids, and they liked the neighborhood and neighbors. The purchase became about more than the final price. While this was happening on his purchasing end, he also used the same strategy on the selling end. His family left notes to potential buyers in the house telling them about the special aspects of the house and the neighborhood. They made the purchase something that wasn't one-sided for the buyers.

They took the perspective of the others involved in the transaction.

With whom would you rather do business? A person who doesn't care about your outcome? Or a person who is invested in you getting your interest met? The answer is obvious.

This brings us back to the concept of the "interest" in negotiation. I went through a lot of sales training before I started my academic study. Sales training always talks about filling needs, finding wants or desires. Showing people how you can impact the ROI. None of this addresses the underlying interest in a negotiation. Most sales training programs are very surface level. What can you do to make a deal? My student could have dropped the price of his house in California to make a deal or caved to all the demands of the seller in Texas. But that's zero-sum thinking, and it's a win-lose strategy.

What he did was to think about the underlying reason why someone would enter a negotiation to buy or sell each of the houses. The sellers of the home in Texas had neighbors they cared about, a community that was important, and a house that was part of that community. The underlying interest in their move was to achieve the outcome of moving, while also maintaining the community that was important to them. Would they want to sell the house to someone who low-balled them? Or lied in the negotiation? No.

Meanwhile he was trying to sell his own house in California. He prepared well, with strong positions that facilitated achievement of his underlying interest—moving his family successfully, both socially and financially, to Texas. And even though he would probably never see the buyers of his house again, he wanted them to leave them feeling they had also achieved their interests. It's not always easy to do this. Often people don't come to the negotiating table with a clear understanding of their interests, and they need some help to determine them.

It's not enough to know your reason for being in the negotiation; you have to be willing to give on your positions to achieve your interest. I always tell prospective negotiators, "Hold your interests tightly, but hold your positions loosely."

Many negotiators have a difficult time loosely holding to their positions. The positions are salient and measurable—they are easy. In the house buying example, it's very easy to hold on to the price of the house—even when you are a seasoned negotiator who is aware of interests. I recently looked at a house that was very interesting to me. It had one problem: there wasn't enough family space. The bedrooms were great, the kitchen was great. The living room and dining room were restrictively small. The price was competitive. And I liked the house. It had everything that I wanted, except the room for my family to all be together in the family space. In fact, the dining area was so small that my immediate family couldn't all eat at the same time. Not what I want for my Thanksgiving dinner.

The realtor asked me why I didn't want to make an offer, and I told her my concerns. Then I said, "It's a great house and maybe if the price were lower…" She's a good realtor and said, "You won't get what you want from this house, no matter the price. We're not going to offer on it." And that snapped me back to reality. Wow, it sure is easy to get hung up on the positions. And when we get hung up on positions, we end up in a lose-lose scenario. Could I get this house for a lower price? Probably. But the compromise is the seller gives up some of their profit and maybe that impacts what they can buy, and they don't achieve their interests. And the compromise for me is that I don't achieve my interest of a home that is comfortable for my wife, my children, and me. Everyone loses on the deal.

When we hold onto positions too tightly or look for the compromise, we lose. On the other hand, when we look for the collaborative outcome and take everyone's interests into account, we can do better.

In a recent discussion with my class, we talked about this at great length. There is a very strong pull to focus on the positions in a negotiation, and this is especially apparent when the negotiation is an organizational negotiation. What I mean by "organizational negotiation" is any negotiation that is driven or set by your organization. I come from a background in sales. Many of the negotiations that I've undertaken had positions that were set for me by my organization. The sales goal, or quota, was set by the sales manager, the maximum discount was set by someone in the finance department, the promotional price set by the marketing department. This leads to a lot of positional bargaining. And realistically, it leads away from the reason we are negotiating in the first place.

This is one reason that sales professionals get a bad reputation. There is no meaning behind the positions.

One of my students asked during the discussion, *"How can I negotiate well when I don't have any passion for what I am negotiating?"* Great question. But I don't necessarily think it's passion; I think it's meaning. In the example above, with three different departments impacting, or even determining the positions and no connection to a purpose, how can someone represent that well?

I worked mostly in small companies or start-up companies. We had a clear purpose most of the time: survival. As a small company just starting out, it was up to the few salespeople to ensure that the bills could be paid, the salaries met, and the growth maximized. I often say that it was up to the salespeople to make sure everyone in the company could eat. And at a couple of the organizations, that was no exaggeration.

That brings us back to the "why" in the negotiation. Why are you even involved in the negotiation? The question that I ask to help focus negotiators is, *Why are you in the room?* It helps you lean into the underlying interest in a negotiation. If the focus is solely on positions, it becomes a haggling situation.

Imagine you go to your boss's office to ask for that eight percent raise. You have thought about the effort that you have been putting in, the extended projects that you have championed, and the growth of your department. You've formulated your argument, and you present it to her. She says, *"You're right. You have been performing at a high level, but due to the economic forces on the organization, I don't have the budget to give you more than three percent at this time."*

If you are focused on the position, you are now in a haggling situation. You will counter with six-and-a-half percent, she will counter with four percent. It will go on until both parties have given up something that they didn't want to give up. You will walk out of her office feeling underappreciated. She will put through your smaller raise feeling exploited at worst or harboring a negative view of a good employee at best.

But why were you seeking the raise in the first place?

What if you approach it with that "why" at the forefront of your negotiation? *"I have been involved in a lot of the extra growth in the department, and I want some recognition for that. I think an eight percent raise is warranted."* Slight difference. You put your why into the initial argument. You want recognition. Now, when the manager says, well, the budget won't allow for eight percent, but I could give you three percent rather than haggling, you can start expanding the outcome. Three percent and a promotion to team lead with a commitment to revisit the raise in six months. Three percent in the raise, plus a one-time bonus. Three percent plus the flexible work schedule that I've been asking about.

Without the why, we get stuck on our positions. And it's worse if we don't know the why.

When it comes to the salesperson with all the positions given to him by the organization, how can he have a clear understanding about why he is negotiating with a customer, if he doesn't understand what's behind the positions?

Good organizations need to be clear and specific in communicating the "why" to those who are negotiating. For the salespeople, why do we charge a premium price? Are we trying to attract customers who fit a certain demographic? Are we trying to position ourselves in the marketplace to connect with a certain type of investor? Do we have a unique product? Do we want to maximize that unique nature before another product erodes our market share?

These questions speak to the student's question, *"How can I negotiate something if I'm not passionate about it?"* You don't have to be passionate; you have to understand why.

Remember, the term that we use in negotiation to describe "why" is Interest, not to be confused with passion. I worked for companies that produced and sold office furniture, engineering software, office software, and software for software development. Was I passionate about those products? Are most people passionate about their work?

Understanding the why opens the door to achieving better outcomes. This can be applied to every negotiation. The hard part is getting to that "why."

In his book *Never Split the Difference*, famous hostage negotiator Chris Voss wrote about a woman who "needed to extract concessions while improving the relationship." No easy task, right? Look at the words he used to describe negotiation! "Concessions must be extracted"? Like a hostage from enemy clutches? He described it as not easy—and a task. We all dread tasks.

When you frame your human interactions so negatively, negotiation becomes something to be dreaded.

Our negotiations (and every human interaction) happen because we can gain so much more from interacting than we can on our own. Frame it as a possible gain, and that will impact what we can achieve. But we will get to that in a later chapter. Right now, we need to focus on loosening our grip on positions to maximize the gain.

Positions only represent one possible way to achieve our interests, our "why." There are other ways out there to get interests met. Some are better, some not quite as good. Some are obvious, and some may not be easy to see. What we can count on is that the people with whom we are negotiating have different information than we do, which leads to different possible positions and different ways to satisfy your interests. We should be willing to listen to others about potential ways to get our interests met.

Ask yourself, *Why am I in the room?* If your answer is only about positions, you aren't ready to negotiate. If your answer is about winning, you aren't ready to negotiate. If you can only see your own positions as the potential outcomes, you aren't ready to negotiate. If you can't articulate a way to benefit the other parties involved in the negotiation, you aren't ready to negotiate.

But if you have a clear idea about your interests and the ability to articulate them, you're ready.

A good negotiator needs to stand for something. Holding on tightly to your interests is firm ground.

Your interest, your "why," is not something that you should compromise. This is where you can stand strong. Balance is for people who don't know who they are. We don't need balance in our business relationships. We need to stand for something. That means that some of your business relationships may no longer be viable. That's ok. When you start to compromise your standards and beliefs to gain something for the organization, integrity goes out the window.

When you are willing to ask some questions and do some preparation, it can change a lot about the process of the negotiation. One thing that won't change is the ambiguity of the process. Humans typically don't like ambiguous situations. We do a lot to remove ambiguity in our lives, sometimes even following a negative path because that's better than not knowing.

But we can become more comfortable with ambiguity. It takes practice, patience, and time, but in the long run, it is the better way to negotiate.

One of the most intimidating things that happens in a negotiation is when we feel like we don't have all the necessary information. We prepare for the negotiation, we think we're set, and we walk into a surprise. We realize that the other parties involved in the negotiation have different information, and it's really intimidating and makes it difficult to move forward.

Have you ever negotiated with somebody and surprised them? Many will train you that shock is an opportunity. They will train you to take advantage of the situation, to push at this point of weakness.

Now add in ambition. Most people who study negotiation have some level of ambition. There would be no reason to study if it were otherwise. If we are astute observers of the world, we know that driven people are seldom driven to be good.

So, the combination of being driven in an

ADDRESSING AMBIGUITY

chapter 8

ambiguous situation can lead to a lot of opportunities to try and take advantage of the people and situation.

This is one course of action that I definitively don't recommend, for one reason: Eventually, you're going to be that person who was surprised or caught off guard. If you have used this against people in your business life, those same people will use it against you. If you have a reputation as an opportunistic negotiator, people will be opportunistic against you.

Several students in my class were recently faced with this dilemma in the job market. One student came to me with his situation. He did an internship with a company that he really liked. At the end of the internship, he was offered a job. It seemed great. He liked the company, and the work, and there was a lot of opportunity for growth. I asked him what was behind his hesitation. Was it the salary? Benefits? Location? "No," he said, all those aspects were great. But he had applied to grad school. He had a plan to attend grad school before he had taken the internship. So, now he was faced with the ambiguity—he could take the full-time job, or he could wait to hear from grad school, which wasn't guaranteed. This wasn't how he envisioned his future. Ambiguity with both decisions.

This is a very common occurrence with students. They have interviews and internships, and from those they get job offers. But there's a catch. They get an offer that wants an answer. Usually, the time frame is a couple weeks. One student told me they gave her 24 hours to accept. In addition, the students often have interviews that are scheduled in the future. To accept a job early would be to forgo the interviews in the future. And because human nature drives us, a lot see those future interviews as more desirable. It's not that the companies or the jobs are better, but we have a tendency to build up the possibility until the concrete details are put in place. This is a lot of ambiguity for a college senior to endure.

Let's think about why organizations do that to students. Why would you tell a college senior, 21 years old, who has likely never made a bigger decision, *I need an answer to this offer in the next 24 hours, or even two weeks?*

The organizations are trying to reduce ambiguity as well. They have staffing needs, budgets to make, and strategic planning that needs to be done. This strategy of the exploding offer, as it's called, is a tool to try and get to a resolution to ambiguity as quickly as possible.

This means there are two competing ambiguity reduction desires. The students and the organization can feel like they are at odds.

But are they really at odds? What is causing this situation? Let's pull back the curtain and try to find the origin of the stress.

The students are finishing college, a commitment that averages five years and costs over $50,000 a year at the institution where I teach. They want a job. They want a good job. When they feel pressured into a decision, no matter how good the job is, the satisfaction with that job goes down. This can lead to premature turnover, reduced performance, and other issues in the early career.

The desire to reduce ambiguity can lead to another strategy that exacerbates the problem even more. Students, in an attempt to reduce their ambiguity, are accepting jobs and **continuing to interview** with the plan to take a better offer if they get one. Be sure that you're clear about this. Students are working around the companies' ambiguity reduction strategy by accepting jobs, knowing they will rescind the acceptance if a future offer is better for them.

That doesn't do much good for the companies who are trying to reduce their ambiguity. I think this is one of the drivers of the phenomenon of the 24-hour exploding offer. Companies are no longer willing to wait two weeks for a student when they know the commitment may not hold.

It doesn't do much for the students either. It damages reputation, and it builds a sense of distrust with organizational life. Students are already coming from a big organization (the University) that can make them feel like an insignificant part of what's going on. That shouldn't be something that carries on into their next organization.

Similarly, organizations should be there to maximize the experience for employees, just as they want the employees to maximize the outcomes for them. This interdependence should lead to a better experience, but oftentimes, both parties in this long-term negotiation are hesitant to accept the ambiguity and do what they can to minimize it.

Another reason to take this seriously and cautiously is because the student is developing a reputation as a negotiator. And reputation follows you. We live in a very connected world, and if we take advantage of someone else, whether in a business situation or personal, people hear about it. People know us, particularly if we are in an industry that is very well-connected. Even if not, people will know us by our reputation. There aren't too many jobs that allow a person to hide from their reputation. Most jobs today collect metrics, collect feedback, collect KPIs, and collect so much data, and that becomes the basis for reputation. And if it were that simple, reputation probably wouldn't be an issue because they would be accurate.

But think of the many times you've called a customer service line. Sometimes, the person on the other end is amazing and helpful; sometimes, they are terrible. After the terrible interaction, you get an automated email asking you to review your experience, and you can post it to Google Reviews or some other online site. You write, "Terrible customer service" or something to that effect and give them the dreaded one star. You just impacted the reputation of that company. The research tells us that when we don't have first-hand experience with a company we rely heavily on the reviews of others. You also impacted the reputation of the customer service agent on the other end of the phone or chat.

You may be thinking, great, that was the goal. Before you jump to that end, let's think about a couple of issues with this process. First, is your review an accurate reflection of the customer service at that organization? Maybe you caught someone on a bad day. Maybe he has a sick child at home and was up all night caring for her? Maybe it's just as simple as a bad day at work. Haven't you had a bad day at work? Do you want to be judged for your worst performance? Or your best? Our reputation shouldn't be built only from a negative interaction, but responding with a review that trashes a company for a single bad interaction does just that.

That leads me to the next issue. We need to be more holistic in our interactions. If you are on the phone with customer service or tech support, you are probably having a bad day, too. The research indicates that when we are in a negative mood, it changes how information gets processed in our brains. That negative mood moves us to process information in a different part of the brain. We don't process in the pre-frontal cortex; we process in the amygdala. This is the fight or flight center of the brain. We are not processing to solve a complex issue. *"How do I get my issue resolved with customer service?"* Instead, we are processing it as "I am here to fight for my resolution," which leads to a very different interaction.

This leads me to the final issue: are you impacting this person's reputation and this organization's reputation in the way you want or should, given your own emotional state?

Now that you know about the impact of our emotional state on the decision-making process, are there any reviews that you want to take back? I'm not trying to shame you for past reviews; I know the research, and I have reviews that I would like to take back and reputations that I would like to help repair. But now that you know the research, you may think twice before you let someone have it in an online forum or on a review site.

Let me give you one example of this and how it could be managed. I am a guitar player, and I have a guitar that was built by a smaller builder in California. (I'm going to give you the name because I have a lot of respect for this person and the way he runs his business.) Chad Jennings owns and operates Jennings Guitars, and it enjoys a good reputation. I wanted to buy a replacement part for my guitar, a replacement pickguard. So, I emailed Chad and asked about the part. He told me that they were about to place an order with their vendor and then passed along the price. I emailed back that the price was acceptable, and I would love to get the part as soon as possible. "No problem. I'll email you with a link to pay and input your shipping address when it arrives."

A couple of months passed. I have to admit that I wasn't so happy with Chad. I emailed again. No answer. I waited a couple weeks and emailed again. As you can imagine, I was getting more frustrated since the original discussion was that the order was being placed and my part would be included.

This happened near the end of the pandemic. I live in Texas, and we weren't distancing or wearing masks anymore, but Chad lives in California, and they were still in the thick of it. Additionally, the pandemic hit his small shop pretty hard, and he had recently been sick and recovering. I didn't have any of this information, but I did have the reputation that Chad had built in the guitarist community. He was well known for his dedication to his customers.

Knowing his reputation, I could imagine there must be some extenuating circumstances, so I emailed again.

This time, I got a response from Chad asking for my shipping address, which I sent to him. Two days later, a package arrived from Jennings Guitars with the part and a handwritten note from Chad explaining the situation. I'm not a famous guitar player, and Chad isn't the biggest guitar builder; it could have been a negative interaction for both of us. He had no reason to send me the part at no charge. He didn't gain anything from me. But in this instance, both parties took some time to understand the other party before responding with a negative reaction.

Apply this to your business interactions. When the purchasing agent says, *I just can't pay that much*, how would your interaction change if you took some time to understand the circumstances? Instead of immediately updating your offer, what if you changed to a mindset that focused on the others' outcomes as well as yours? That looks like asking questions first and trying to understand, not to overpower. Can you tell me about your constraints?

Is this a budget issue or a timing issue? How does this impact you in your organization? (Your salary? Your bonus? Your annual review?)

What about applying this to your home? Imagine how you could change your interactions at home if you didn't spend your energy trying to make counteroffers but rather trying to understand the interests and reasons of the others involved. When we take the time to understand those interests, we can make counteroffers that make sense.

Think again of the purchasing agent who says no to your proposal. Typically, there would be another offer at a lower price. "Well, if you can't do $12.50 per unit, how about $11.75?" Without an understanding of the issue, you've just reset the maximum that this person will pay. You have given a concession that might not be a concession that moves you toward an agreement. We want every concession to move us toward agreement.

This brings us back to reputation. If I give concessions that don't provide value, I'm building a reputation that's not connected to value. I'm just another salesperson trying to get his price. However, if I ask the questions and determine where the value is held, I build a reputation as the person who brings value to the table. If I consistently bring value, I'm the first phone call each time you need something. Trust is built, and that means every interaction gets easier and easier, and the value goes up because I spend less time building each successful transaction. When we do business, I don't have to work to install proxies for trust because we have already built trust—it was built when I started showing true concern for your outcomes.

We're all coming from different positions, we have different goals, different values, ideas, and biases. When we're negotiating for daily outcomes, our subconscious biases typically are helpful. I went to a restaurant the second week that I lived in Waco and got sick. I haven't been back in eighteen years, even though a lot of people tell me it's great and they have really good food. The one time I went I got sick, so now I have a bias and I won't go back. Reputation is powerful. One bad experience is hard to recover from.

Coupled with all this is confirmation bias, that is a bias toward the information that supports our position. If I hold the position and I see only the information that supports my position, that's confirmation bias. The way to combat that is to seek out other sources of information that tell me something different or from a different point of view, then take that information, synthesize it, and grow from there.

The next bias is anchoring, the tendency to heavily weight information that we receive early in the process. This bias is very commonly used in negotiation by giving the first offer. If I give the first offer, very often that anchors the discussion. This is why when you drive onto a car lot there's already a price hanging in the window, or when you look at a house there's already a listing price. These are first offers, and they're meant to make you think the value of that item is connected to that number. The best way to address anchoring is to have a clear strategy about offers and concessions before you go into the negotiation.

Next, the overconfidence bias is placing too much faith in your own skills or knowledge. This often happens with people who have done specific negotiations over and over. If you've been involved in the same sales cycle, many times the overconfidence bias can lead you to prepare less and be more dependent on thinking on your feet. This impacts the strategy you employ.

The gambler's fallacy tells us that past events are predictors of future events. An example is if you flip a coin seven times and it lands on heads seven times in a row. The gambler's fallacy would say it's going to be heads on the next flip. The gambler's fallacy could also say I'm due for tails. However, every time we flip a coin, it's a discrete independent event, and you have the same probability of heads or tails on every flip, regardless of the previous flip.

In successful negotiations, multiple factors influence the outcome. However, a key predictor of success lies in adopting a deliberate strategy to collaborate. Additionally, meticulous follow-through on the preparations proves to be crucial. A common hindrance to successful negotiations is the fundamental attribution error, the inclination to blame others when things go awry. Overcoming this requires adopting an objective perspective. Instead of assigning failure to specific negotiation participants, it is vital to objectively analyze the various contributing factors. This involves examining both positive and negative aspects of our interactions and exploring ways to capitalize on positive elements.

Differences in information and biases are inherent in negotiations, but they need not be perceived negatively. The diversity of information among individuals can be a positive factor, creating opportunities for mutual benefit. Recognizing that each participant brings a unique perspective allows for constructive discussions toward mutual gain in our outcomes. It is crucial to acknowledge that our information is inherently skewed and biased, shaped by our individual paths to success. Allowing that bias to exist allows us to move forward and embrace our differences.

chapter 9

COLLABORATION NOT COMPETITION

The idea of win-win was birthed out of Roger Fisher's seminal book, *Getting to Yes*. In that book, Fisher talked about focusing on the people, not on the problem, focusing on how we can gain together as opposed to gaining individually. He took a lot of the competitive aspects out of negotiation.

Prior to that book, negotiation was a very competitive activity; it was seen as a win-lose proposition. Many of the negotiation trainings looked at how to maximize our own outcome because people viewed negotiation as a zero-sum activity where whatever you gain comes out of my pocket and whatever I gain comes out of your pocket. It's a view of negotiation that defines the interaction as limited and the resources as fixed.

That zero-sum mentality, also called distributive negotiation or competitive negotiation, is what leads us to view our negotiations as a competitive endeavor, as a win proposition. Fisher decided that's not necessarily the best way to achieve outcomes. Through his work and the work of others at the time, the idea of a win-win outcome was created. The win-win outcome means we want to make sure all negotiation parties end up with a win at the end of the negotiation.

This is obviously a much better goal than the win-lose idea. If I go into a negotiation with that win-lose, competitive, or zero-sum idea, we battle, we fight. I'm less willing to give any concessions, or move off of my position. I'm less willing to provide benefit to you because it comes out of my pocket.

I don't like the rhetoric or motives of win-win. I think there is a better way. In this chapter, I'm going to propose an idea that I call "joint gain negotiation." I believe it takes the best of win-win and adds ethical flavor, which maximizes what we can get in our negotiations.

The words we use shape our motives. The motives that we take into the interaction shape our behaviors. We need to be aware and deliberate with what we say and do in our interactions if we are going to achieve better results.

In Chapter One, I noted a study by a professor friend of mine who was interested in win-win decisions. That study was first done with MBA students at Harvard and Northwestern.

If you recall, they were paired, and one person was tasked with making a distribution choice: keep $10 and give your partner $8, or keep $12 and give your partner $20. The researchers found that most of the time, the person tasked with this decision chose to take $10 and give their partner $8.

This study reveals the problem with the win-win model. Both participants have more money than they did before the game. Thus, both outcomes are a win-win. But, most people, in most cases, including those who took this study, view the outcome in which a counterpart gets a greater benefit as a loss—even though they also receive more.

In case you think this was a "one-off," know that these professors did the research over years with diverse groups of students. These students were also top business leaders. They were admitted to prestigious MBA programs. This study proves what many of us already know: this is how business leaders act.

This study also highlights that winning doesn't mean settling for second place. The person tasked with the decision can either be $10 or $12 richer. Having $12 is more than $10, regardless of what the other party receives. When engaging partners, clients, customers, or suppliers, it is essential to recognize that the term "win-win" requires careful handling. In these scenarios, we aim for the success of all parties involved, as long as their success does not compromise our position or make us appear weak.

In studies examining this phenomenon, researchers noted that deciders were more inclined to share benefits with others when they shared a close, long-standing friendship. However, in the majority of organizational negotiations, most of our interactions involve acquaintances or colleagues we know but with whom we lack a deep, personal bond. Close friendships in most of our work relationships are the exception rather than the rule. In these instances, using the term "win-win" often activates our competitive instincts, pushing us towards a more self-centric mindset.

That's why I propose a redefinition of our approach. Let's shift away from the conventional "win-win" terminology and adopt a perspective centered on "joint gain." By doing so, we can transform our motives. It's essential to understand that the words we use define our world and impact our fundamental motivations. When we emphasize "joint gain," we shift our focus from individual victory to collective benefit. This perspective revolutionizes our entire approach to negotiation.

We live in a world shaped by language and meaning. The term "win" carries specific connotations that heighten our competitive nature, especially in today's context. However, when we adopt a "joint gain" perspective, we realign our motivations. We cease to be driven solely by the desire to triumph personally and instead focus on maximizing the benefits for all parties involved. This change in rhetoric alters our motives profoundly.

Moving from "win-win" to "joint gain" makes us more critical thinkers. It prompts us to seek creative solutions, injecting value into our negotiations, all while preserving ethical conduct. When we negotiate with the aim of maximizing joint gain, we prioritize the interdependence of our objectives. It redefines success, emphasizing that achieving our initial goals is paramount. Anything beyond that represents extra value, which we actively pursue but not at the expense of others.

Adopting this ethical approach can enhance your reputation, relationships, and desirability as a negotiation partner. It's not a one-time strategy; it's a long-term investment. By consistently providing value and focusing on joint gain, you become the negotiator others trust and prefer to work with. This reputation extends beyond individual negotiations; it becomes your brand.

Some may argue that their industries are fiercely competitive, filled with tough suppliers and challenging customers. However, it's crucial to recognize that providing joint gain offers immense power. When you consistently deliver the most value, you wield considerable influence. This approach does not entail giving everything away; it's about ensuring your interests are met while also maximizing joint gain.

The shift from "win-win" to "joint gain" does not undermine your ability to succeed. Quite the opposite; it enhances your prospects of achieving mutually beneficial outcomes. By upholding ethical principles and treating negotiation as a platform for collective benefit, you set the stage for more meaningful and fruitful interactions. Embracing this approach isn't a hindrance; it's a pathway to enduring success.

Some people will think that this view of negotiation, this method of achieving an outcome, is weak. I have been teaching these methods for years to students, from undergraduates to the C-suite, and one of the biggest concerns is that people don't want to appear weak. So, my challenge to you here is: don't appear weak.

Providing value to others doesn't make you weak. Being indecisive, being defensive, having a closed mind—these make you weak. Being unable to consider alternatives makes you weak. Being positional, not sharing information, taking a deal that doesn't benefit everyone involved—these things make you weak.

Working together, sharing relevant information, adjusting expectations, and pushing for the greatest outcome are signs of strength.

As I go through and explain the ideas of joint gain to students or when consulting clients, most can see the logic and the beauty of the idea. Even adding in the Christian elements doesn't usually make people wonder about the process. But when they get to the end, when it comes time to put this ideology into action, people get squeamish and skeptical. The thought process turns to: "If I am so concerned with benefiting others, won't I get taken advantage of?" "If I am so concerned with the outcomes of others, won't my outcome suffer?" "If I am so concerned with others, won't I be viewed as a weak negotiator?"

This is where you need to make a change in your mindset.

I have participated in many sports in my lifetime, both competitive sports and those you played just for fun. Recently, I have been doing some of these sports with my kids. It's rewarding and I want them to get the most out of the experience that they can.

So, that means I can't really take it easy on them. If I'm playing basketball in the driveway with one of my kids and every time they get the ball I let them make an easy layup, they won't get better. I have to apply the appropriate pressure and make them work for it a little to push them to get the most out of the interaction. Recently, I have been lifting weights with my sons (I don't with my daughter because she lifts competitively and none of us can keep up with her). One of our jokes at the gym is that the light weights are a lot easier to lift than the heavy weights. It's a funny dad joke because it's both obvious and motivational. We all know that you don't grow (physically, emotionally, spiritually, etc.) unless you are challenged. So, we lift the heavy weights.

The joint gain process asks you to do the same thing. Take

chapter 10

NOT ALTRUISM

the challenge of pushing those involved in the negotiation. Don't accept bad deals, don't settle for less.

Settle for more.

This is what separates the good negotiator from the great negotiator.

If you want to be the great negotiator in the interaction, you need to take the responsibility to create value. Those who create value become the most desirable partner. If you are the most desirable partner, you are more successful.

Think about this for a minute. Be a critical thinker. With whom do you want to interact? The difficult people? Obviously, no. But sometimes we must work with the difficult people. If you are difficult in return, everything is harder. If you are the desirable negotiation partner, even the difficult people will be happier to work with you. And that will lead to a better process, outcome, relationship, reputation, and ultimately a benefit for all involved.

Be demanding. Be willing to say, "No, we can do better." Don't let others accept less. Make it a practice to ask your negotiation partners if there is a way they can improve their outcomes. And commit to trying to achieve that better for them. The joint gain idea doesn't ask you to be a nice, giving negotiator. It demands that you are tough. It demands you look for more value, better value, and better outcomes. Think about this as the provider role. If you are the main provider for your family unit, doesn't that give you a level of power? In our families, we don't hesitate to make sure that others get great outcomes, but that doesn't diminish the power of the provider.

If you consistently bring value into the negotiation, come up with creative outcomes, and ensure that others benefit, then you have a level of power in that interaction. Many times, in organizational life, people take that power and try to leverage it for individual gain. But what if you leveraged it for joint gain? Think about how that would impact your reputation, trust levels, and relationships. It could be a boon to your business.

And this is consistent with Christian values.

Jesus called us to love others as we love ourselves. Think about how you love yourself. Is it best to take the easy route? Is it best to slack off? Obviously not. We all do it sometimes, but if we want to grow, we can't always lift just the light weights.

If you want to be a great negotiator, you have to demand greatness in your interactions. Greatness is defined by everyone getting more, not a single individual who benefits. Great leaders, managers, musicians, weightlifters, parents, and great people *all* make others better, not just themselves.

Love others the way you love yourself. Look out for them the way you look out for yourself. Benefit them the way you benefit yourself. Be a great negotiator.

To be great, one must have critical thought, creativity, planning, and an openness to others' ideas. It is not easy, but nothing worthwhile is on that easy road.

Ethical Implications

Every individual comes into a negotiation with their own biases, ideas, ethics, and morality. I approach negotiation as I approach the rest of my life, through the lens of Christian ethics. I think whether you're a Christian or not, it will be helpful for you to understand and process the important moral choices you make on a day-to-day basis.

We have spent time considering how to balance Christian faith and successful negotiation. There are difficulties with working in today's organizations and being consistent in applying the principles that we know are ethical and moral. To maintain the standard we have developed and yet maintain the standard of the organization's goals, we may find inconsistencies or difficulties. Again, this flows out of the amoral context of most organizations.

Be vigilant about organizations that claim morality. An organization can't be moral. An organization can't have an ethical stance. Only the people in the organization can have morality or ethics. So, when dealing with an organization that professes to be "Christian," be aware of the individual in front of you. Are his behaviors indicative of a moral negotiator? Is he using ethical tactics?

And this is where the line can get blurry. We use the shield of the organizational stance to cover behaviors and motives. I work for a university that professes a "Christian" morality. It impacts some decisions that are made, but the implementation of those decisions by different people with different ethical frameworks makes for some confusion about the ethical stand of the University. This should be your expectation. The organization itself cannot think, act, or have motives. The people can be guided by the culture but make decisions on a day-to-day basis as to whether they will deviate from the professed culture.

Chick-fil-A has been well known for its corporate stance against homosexuality, right? Chick-fil-A, the organization, used to donate to charitable organizations that were against the LGBTQ agenda. The organization no longer makes those donations. The owner of Chick-fil-A still donates to these organizations. Does that mean that the person working behind the counter at your local restaurant hates gay people? Does it mean they should?

Just because we assign a morality or an ethical stance to an organization doesn't mean that every individual in that organization will live it out the way we think they will. I was on a trip with my boys in New York City. We went to a Chick-fil-A to get lunch. The server handed us our food and said, "Next!" My boys stood there dumbfounded. I knew why. "She didn't say 'My pleasure' when we said thank you…" my son noted as we walked away.

They grew up in Texas and can't imagine that people wouldn't be polite. I grew up in the Midwest and explained to them that she just wanted to make it through her day and serving them might not have been her pleasure, since she was serving the whole of Lower Manhattan. But they had assigned the corporate morality they knew from Chick-fil-A in Texas to everyone that was associated to Chick-fil-A.

How this impacts you in a negotiation is important.

When you enter a negotiation with a pre-conceived notion about how everyone in that organization (or class of individuals, e.g. car salespeople, insurance adjusters, corporate purchasing departments, etc.) is going to act, you will miss out on the opportunity to get to joint gain. You will act positional and closed off and therefore miss out on value from this specific interdependent interaction. Each individual is going to approach the negotiation differently, and if you assign a preconceived morality to them, you miss the opportunity to work with them. Additionally, everyone can be influenced to adopt the joint gain view if you are willing to work for it. And maybe wait for it.

I can hear you thinking, *What about the other side of the interaction? What if you aren't acting in concert with the proclaimed values of the organization? How will that impact the negotiation for you?* Well, you are likely to miss out on some potential creative outcomes.

It comes back to the question of amorality. Most of the time negotiators enter the interaction without an explicit representation of the values they are bringing with them. In fact, that's how most sales programs, negotiation trainings, leadership seminars, and the like would train people. Check your moral stance at the door.

But how does it change the interaction when you come in and say, "You know what, this is an important negotiation for me. I'm not leaving until you and I squeeze every bit of value from this interaction. I'm not leaving until I get what I want, *AND* I'm not leaving until you get what you want. Yes, I want to gain, and I've found that I can usually get more for myself when you get more too. So, I'm not willing to shortchange either one of us. I'm here to settle for more." Be explicit about how you are going to negotiate. State explicitly that you aren't going to accept a bad deal for you, but also that you won't accept a deal that is bad for the others involved.

Imagine the change in my interaction in New York at Chick-fil-A if we had an explicit conversation about how the interaction was going to proceed before we entered it. "I have some hungry boys here, but they are missing

Texas. Do you think you can give them the quintessential southern Chick-fil-A experience?" "Well, I'm tired and there are thousands of people that come through this shop every day. Most of them are not 'Southern' in their interactions, so no. You may think my matter-of-fact attitude is rude, but I can get you some lunch." Now I can decide. Does the chicken sandwich itself fulfill my interest? I could get even deeper in the interaction and ask her about her politics on LGBTQ matters and see where that takes us. If this was going to be a long-term interaction, that may be something that's necessary. If this is a negotiation about a close, ongoing partnership I may want to know about politics. It doesn't mean that if she and I disagreed on LGBTQ issues that we couldn't work together, but we would need to know so we *could* work together.

Mature negotiators can disagree and work together.

The big issue here is that working together, being open and up front about your interests, demanding more in your interactions—none of this is soft negotiating. None of this is just giving.

This is a demanding way to negotiate. This is only for tough negotiators. You can't be weak and use this method. This is always the fear that people bring into this method of negotiation. Will others take advantage of me?

I encourage you to change your mindset. Don't go into your negotiation with that adversarial ideology. Rather, go into it with the idea that you are the provider of value in the negotiation. You are the one that can benefit others. No one can steal something from you if you've already planned to give it to them. Others can't take advantage of you if you've decided you are there to benefit them.

It also changes the interaction. If the others involved in the negotiation see that you are there as a positive force in generating value, it makes it a lot more difficult for them to try and take without giving. Additionally, you need to be willing to give value contingently.

It looks like, "Yes, I can give you that concession, that value you want, that benefit, if…" then you ask for the important aspects of the negotiation that meet your interests.

Oftentimes organizations will have goals that are very positional and short-term in nature. For example, I was in sales before I was an academic and one of the hallmarks of many sales jobs is the quota. Meeting the quota is a very short-term, very positional goal. If I have a quota to make to keep my job or get paid, I'm focused on that over and above the long-term goals, the ethical and moral goals of the organization. The quota puts an unnecessary constraint on my interactions by forcing a focus on the immediate sale. There are a lot of deals that are pursued merely to fill a quota rather than to benefit the others involved.

Organizations exist to achieve different goals than individuals. It's not likely that an individual would produce a smartphone on their own. It's not that it's impossible, but the incentives don't work for the individual. Developing the smartphone is only a benefit with the resources of an organization behind it. Organizations play an important role in setting goals and getting things done. The reason that organizations exist is because humanity benefits from organizing. We get the benefit of ideas and reach. More gets done with organizations. We get smartphones.

This comes with some important boundary conditions that are both upheld and violated by some of the best organizations. We all know organizations that do well aligning their goals with goals of the individuals involved. We probably know organizations that don't do that very well. It's the reason that unions exist. There was a time when the goals of the organization superseded the goals of the individual in such a dramatic way that those individuals stood up to the organization and fought for goal alignment.

Our focus is on the organizational interactions, particularly negotiation. My warning to you is to be deliberate with your ideas, goals, words, and interactions. If you find yourself in a situation where the company goals are leading you in a direction that may be against your own ethics or morals, ask questions. Remember the words of Paul:

"Do nothing from selfish ambition or conceit, but in humility count others more significant than yourselves. Let each of you look not only to his own interests, but also to the interests of others. Have this mind among yourselves, which is yours in Christ Jesus" (Philippians 2:3-5).

There are times we may have to set aside our own selfish ambition for the good of others. Notice that Paul doesn't say, "set aside ambition," but he qualifies it with "selfish." If your ambition is not selfish, you are going down the right path. Determining this is going to take some careful, critical examination.

You may remember this admonition in his letter to the Galatians,

"A man reaps what he sows. Whoever sows to please their flesh, from the flesh will reap destruction; whoever sows to please the Spirit, from the Spirit will reap eternal life. Let us not become weary in doing good, for at the proper time we will reap a harvest if we do not give up. Therefore, as we have opportunity, let us do good to all people, especially to those who belong to the family of believers" (Galatians 6:7-10).

We, as Christians, need to be aware of the impact of our actions. Will we trade a short-term, one-time gain for a compromise of our morality?

"Well, it's business" is the argument. My rebuttal? Big deal. I don't care if it's business, personal, or family. Why would a different morality apply? Does Paul say to set aside selfish ambition with your family, but cut the throats of those in the marketplace? No, he doesn't.

Didn't Jesus turn over tables in the temple and throw people out because they were cheating their customers? He did. (See Matthew 21:12, Luke 19:45, Mark 11:15-17.) This story is important enough to be recorded in three of the gospels.

"It's just business" is not an excuse to give up your ethics and morality. In fact, you should hold yourself to a higher standard in your business dealings. Don't be the same as everyone. Christians were sent into the world so that through us, He is known. We are supposed to be different. We are supposed to be in the world, not of the world.

> *"I have given them your word, and the world has hated them because they are not of the world, just as I am not of the world. I do not ask that you take them out of the world, but that you keep them from the evil one. They are not of the world, just as I am not of the world. Sanctify them in the truth; your word is truth. As you sent me into the world, so I have sent them into the world"* (John 17:14-18).

We are in the world to shine a light on the Truth. Doing business in a questionable way, whether it is acceptable in society or not, is against our calling as Christians. Do not fool yourself. The smallest compromises in ethics, the smallest cracks in character, lead to dire consequences.

> *"Then the Lord said to Cain, 'Why are you angry? Why is your face downcast? If you do what is right, will you not be accepted? But if you do not do what is right, sin is crouching at your door; it desires to have you, but you must rule over it'"* (Genesis 4:6-7).

> *"You have heard that it was said, 'Eye for eye, and tooth for tooth.' But I tell you, do not resist an evil person. If anyone slaps you on the right cheek, turn to them the other cheek also. And if anyone wants to sue you and take your shirt, hand over your coat as well. If anyone forces you to go one mile, go with them two miles. Give to the one who asks you, and do not turn away from the one who wants to borrow from you"* (Matthew 5:38-42).

Now consider this question: With whom do you want to do business?

In my classes I teach the importance of being "the most desirable partner" in a negotiation. This means different things to different people. That's ok. People are idiosyncratic; the differences are why we study psychology, sociology, and business processes. But we must be a partner that is seen as desirable.

Some of the desirability comes from context. If you have a product that fills a need and doesn't have a competitor in the marketplace, you are in a different situation than an established market with many choices. But it doesn't absolve you of ethics, morals, and common decency.

For instance. I worked for a start-up that had a unique piece of software. Our product allowed the engineers to shave significant time from the process of conceptual idea to finished model in the CAD (Computer Aided Design) software. There were no competitors to the product. We were alone in the marketplace. And you may be thinking, *Well that's a great deal of power. You can set the price; you can control the sales process.*

We could save companies a great deal of money. And I watched my vice president of sales on the phone with one of my customers telling them if they didn't send a purchase order that day, we wouldn't sell to them. It was the end of the quarter, the customer was interested in buying the software, and the VP needed the sale to hit his quota. He offered a discount if they sent a purchase order that day. They said it wasn't a possibility, they were a government agency and needed the right departments to sign off. It took time. They wanted to buy but needed to work it through their system. So, my VP threatened them.

Before you get self-righteous on me and say, *I would never do that*, ask yourself if you have ever used scarcity, whether real or fabricated, to try and sell a product or service? *Act now, or you'll miss out!* It may not be as blatant a threat, but that's what it is. You will miss out if you don't act now is a threat.

This is a common and widely accepted way to do business. That doesn't make it a good way to do business.

Who would you rather work with? *"Oh, I understand the government has a process to get purchases made. How can I work with you to support that process?"* or *"We can't wait for your process; this is a limited time price. The cost goes up next quarter."* Which of these is more likely to get a second call from the customer?

You always want to be the most desirable partner.

The trick is, how do you do that? There is no step-by-step process. There is no method that you need to employ. This is where you need a clear understanding of your interest in the negotiation, and you need to hold that interest tightly. You need to advocate to get your interest met, not your position or your interest. AND you need to advocate that the others in the negotiation get their interests met as well.

We, the best negotiators, are not giving something away for nothing in the negotiation. We are giving away anything we can to get our interests met. We are giving concessions in a deliberate way to move us to the most desirable outcome. We are following a plan that protects our interest, holding our interests tightly but holding our positions loosely. And releasing those positions when that moves us closer to the ultimate interest.

Negotiation often presents us with moral dilemmas. We find ourselves grappling with decisions that pit our personal goals against the well-being of those involved, especially when significant rewards or consequences are at stake. A recent study published in the Harvard Business Review delved into the prevalence of deception in negotiations. The findings were striking. As the potential rewards increased, people became more inclined to bend the truth or withhold information. In a controlled laboratory study, as many as sixty-nine percent of participants resorted to dishonesty when faced with substantial rewards. Surprisingly, even with relatively minor incentives, forty-one percent of participants chose to lie to attain their objectives. This highlights a critical issue. When we perceive an opportunity to achieve our goals, even if the rewards are small, it becomes tempting to compromise our ethical boundaries.

This brings us to a question often posed: how can we reconcile our Christian ethics with the demands of everyday negotiations? It's a real and complex challenge that warrants careful consideration. Striking a balance between achieving desired outcomes and upholding our ethical principles is crucial.

In negotiations, each party typically enters the discussion with a limited view of the situation. We possess only partial information, aware of what we know but ignorant of what others know. This narrow perspective often leads to decisions that prioritize our interests while overlooking the broader context. This myopic approach hinders consistency in our negotiation style and ethical conduct. Consistency is essential because it enables us to uphold ethical standards reliably. It allows those we negotiate with to understand our principles, fostering trust and resulting in more productive interactions.

The foundation of our ethical standards may vary from person to person, influenced by individual beliefs and values. However, some universal principles can guide our ethical conduct. One such principle is the recognition of human dignity, as advocated in 1 Peter 2. This principle encourages us to treat everyone involved in negotiations with honor and respect, irrespective of their similarity to us, their role, or their position in the organization. This concept of human dignity extends to family negotiations, where longstanding relationships sometimes lead to neglecting this vital aspect.

1 Peter 2 further urges us to live as free individuals while refraining from using this freedom as a cover for wrongdoing. It emphasizes the importance of maintaining ethical conduct even when we have the freedom to choose otherwise. This perspective underscores our responsibility to conduct ourselves in a manner that honors God.

A pertinent example of ethical behavior is found in the scripture when it mentions that when reviled, Christ did not respond with reviling. Similarly, when he suffered, he did not resort to threats. Despite the behavior of others, we have the capacity to respond with kindness, fairness, and respect. It also emphasizes that we can remain firm in pursuing our interests without resorting to unethical tactics.

In 1 John 4, we are reminded to love one another, emphasizing that God is love. This love should guide our interactions and negotiations. It doesn't imply capitulating or giving up our objectives. Instead, it suggests that even in the pursuit of our interests, we can demonstrate kindness, understanding, and positivity. We can adhere to the principle of treating others as we wish to be treated, ensuring that our actions align with our Christian values.

Maintaining ethical consistency in negotiations is not synonymous with surrendering our goals. It means negotiating in a manner that aligns with our moral principles while pursuing our interests. We can be firm and assertive in advocating for our objectives while being fair, respectful, and considerate. This approach builds trust and fosters a cooperative atmosphere, ultimately leading to more substantial, sustainable outcomes.

Negotiating ethically does not jeopardize our ability to succeed. On the contrary, it enhances our chances of achieving mutually beneficial results. By prioritizing ethical conduct and treating others with dignity, we pave the way for collaborative, interdependent negotiations that generate value for all parties involved. Maintaining ethical consistency should not be seen as an obstacle but as a path to more meaningful and fruitful negotiations.

As we dive deeper into how to maximize the outcome in each interaction, we need to consider the power of the individuals involved. Much has been written about power in our interactions and daily negotiations. People point to everything from *The Art of War* by Sun Tzu to *The Prince* by Nicolo Machiavelli as authority when it comes to the use of power. We will examine some of that information in this chapter, with a critical eye toward using power to maximize outcomes.

Much of what has been written in the past about power in negotiations focuses on gaining leverage, using power to dominate others, or constraining information. This chapter, as you may have guessed by now, will focus differently on the use of power.

Power in our interactions and relationships has short-term applications, but it also has long-term implications. Let's keep both of those in mind as we consider some of the research that can be applied to our daily situations.

Typically, we think about using our power and influence to push someone in a direction that they don't want to go. But I want you to approach power differently. There is an opportunity for another perspective. Roger Fisher tells us that the most important skill for a negotiator is the ability to take the perspective of the others involved. What if you thought about power from the perspective of your negotiation partner?

chapter 11

POWER AND PERSUASION

The desire for power in negotiation is widespread; those who possess it often seek more. When appropriately wielded, power can serve as a valuable tool for guiding and educating participants in negotiations. However, its most critical function lies in creating value within the negotiation process.

To better comprehend this concept, let's explore the essence of power in negotiation. Possessing power implies control—control over resources, information, or the ability to influence outcomes positively. Typically, individuals with power have something of value. Unfortunately, common practice often sees power being used to exert influence or compel agreement through threats, which is an approach I discourage. Extensive research on leveraging power in negotiations has revealed that such tactics typically lead to suboptimal outcomes. When faced with a negotiator that is trying to use power to force an outcome, research tells us that the others involved in the negotiation become defensive, positional, and closed off to creative outcomes.

In our pursuit of understanding outcomes, it's crucial to expand our perspective. Outcomes extend beyond immediate gains, such as securing a raise, acquiring a customer, or achieving specific operational changes. We should focus on long-term considerations, such as whether this negotiation partner will return for future discussions or whether they will recommend us to others based on their positive experience. Empowering people to share their stories of how we enhanced their negotiation outcomes is where real power lies, not in coercion or manipulation, but in enhancing interactions for everyone involved.

Real power manifests when one utilizes their influence and resources to enrich the negotiation process. It involves improving knowledge, sharing information, and ultimately, enhancing the final outcomes. Real power entails providing valuable resources and opportunities that leave a lasting impression on negotiation participants, thereby fostering trust and solidifying relationships.

In negotiation, we have several opportunities to employ power effectively.

Both power and influence can be harnessed to benefit all parties involved. It is crucial to emphasize that while we seek to achieve our goals in negotiation, we should also work towards enhancing the outcomes for others. This dual approach maximizes the potential for productive and sustainable interactions.

A "low power situation" is how we describe when we find ourselves in a position of lower power in a negotiation. Paradoxically, low power can provide us with a degree of freedom that those in positions of hierarchical or resource-based power may lack. Individuals with lower power often have the creative latitude to explore novel negotiation methods, revise their approach, and reimagine the negotiation process. They can change how outcomes are perceived, introduce new negotiation partners, and expand the pie of resources in innovative ways. They possess the opportunity to engage in negotiations with a broader, more creative mindset.

Moreover, individuals with lower power can focus more intently on their underlying interests rather than rigidly clinging to positional stances. Interests are the driving forces behind why we negotiate. In a low power position, negotiators are more able to abandon unproductive positions and return to their core interests. This adaptability is a hallmark of effective negotiation in lower power scenarios.

Successful individuals in business and negotiation share a common trait: they uplift those they work with. They prioritize not just their individual success but also the success of others, those inside their own organizations, outside their organizations—even their competitors. In both professional and personal negotiations, fostering collaboration and building up others is essential. Whether negotiating with family members, colleagues, or subordinates, the focus should always be on elevating everyone involved.

Consider the actions of exceptional leaders and negotiators. They invest in the success of their counterparts, fostering an environment where everyone can thrive. True power lies in empowering others, not in using power to impose one's will. In personal and professional contexts, working with individuals who prioritize collective success and personal growth is far more rewarding than dealing with those who seek to dominate or control.

This perspective on power deviates from the notion of competitive arousal, a phenomenon deeply embedded in our lives. Competitive arousal is the impulse that pushes us to action in a competitive environment, driving us to achieve specific goals. In contemporary society, we frequently encounter competitive situations, from work targets and personal objectives to fitness goals and competitive sports. However, the key distinction is that in most scenarios, survival is not at stake, but rather, we are striving to excel.

In negotiation, competitive arousal can lead to zero-sum thinking and an inclination towards distributive strategies, which focus on claiming a larger share of limited resources. While competitiveness is not inherently negative, it is essential to understand that we no longer need to defeat others to succeed. Instead, we can embrace a collaborative approach that involves building others up, promoting cooperation, and sharing information and resources. By doing so, we can achieve a competitive edge that goes beyond traditional win-lose dynamics.

The concept of power in negotiation extends far beyond coercion and competition. Real power resides in the ability to enrich the negotiation process for all parties involved, fostering long-term benefits, trust, and fruitful relationships. Whether in positions of high or low power, individuals can employ their influence to create value, prioritize collective success, and depart from competitive zero-sum thinking. By adopting this mindset, negotiators can unlock the full potential of power in negotiations, ultimately achieving more productive and sustainable outcomes.

You have probably had bosses who are both good and bad, maybe they were the same person, different day. The difference can often be boiled down to use of power. We usually refer to this as "leadership." Often, when people talk about leadership, they are referring to the use of power.

Those they see as "leaders" use power to build others up. Those who "lack leadership" typically use power to enhance their own positions and outcomes.

Apply that to a negotiation context. Those who are seen as great negotiators tend to build up others, bring greater resources to the table, get creative outcomes, are excellent problem solvers, and ensure that benefits flow to everyone involved. It doesn't mean they focus only on their own outcomes. It also doesn't mean they don't focus on their own outcomes. Proper use of power gets interests met across the board.

chapter 12

Interdependence is the key to it all. Negotiation only works through interdependence. Whether done well or done poorly, negotiation demands interdependent parties.

Most of our interactions with people require us to either extend interdependence to them or accept interdependence from them. Interdependence means that each individual brings value to the interaction. Interdependence is the value that we can gain by adding others to the interaction. This is the whole being greater than the sum of the parts.

Think of it like a band. The guitar sounds great alone; drums sound great on their own, and each instrument produces music. But it's only when each instrument joins the band that something extraordinary can be produced. In the best bands, each instrument is played by a musician who knows when to be subordinate to the others.

The same happens in negotiations. In many of the interactions that we undertake, we could achieve an outcome on our own, but it wouldn't be the best outcome. In fact, it would be the minimal outcome. We negotiate because that's how we get more. We cannot gain if there's no interdependence. In most of our negotiations and interactions, interdependence is a choice.

I give the same example in class every year. I choose interdependence with my children. I have older children; they are self-sufficient. They contribute to the household. They have some chores, and they get some benefits from being part of the family. We don't have explicit interdependence though. I don't make them complete a chore to earn time on the internet, food, or shelter. Rather, they get the benefits and I ask them to complete the tasks. We have an agreement in place that I, as their father, will provide for them, not just basic needs, but also benefits. In return they will provide for the family by doing

INTERDEPENDENCE

dishes, yardwork, and taking care of the dog. We all choose this interdependence. I could make demands and withhold rewards to get them to do the chores, but that's not the best way to get things done. Instead, I explain to them the value of their work to the bottom line of the household.

Think about different bosses or subordinates. Think about different organizational cultures of which you have been a part. Which have been a joy, and which have been a pain? Do you like working for a boss who demands and directs? Do you like working with a boss who invites and engages? This is very connected to the use of power discussion from the previous chapter. Those with more power may make the choice for interdependence.

I know what the research tells us. We all want to be part of the decision-making process. We are more engaged, more committed when we are included.

Interdependence is a choice.

It goes both ways. My children can choose an interdependent relationship, just as I can. We can meet and choose to work together. Or, individually, we can decide to fight. We can make the interaction about who wins. My kids can decide not to do dishes after they are asked. I can turn the internet off or take the car keys until they do chores.

In your organizations you can make the same choices.

Those you work with can make the same choices.

Will you be in competition? Will you adopt a scarcity mindset?

The previous chapters of this book have been dedicated to the science behind joint gain, so the concept should be familiar to you. Let me add some of the spiritual aspects to this idea. I'm going to use a story from Nehemiah that doesn't get a lot of attention.

The Jews were in exile. The Persians had taken them out of the land of Israel and spread them around the empire. This was standard procedure to try and assimilate a conquered people. One of the Jews was a man named Nehemiah. He had risen to a place of incredible power in the court of

Artaxerxes. He was his cupbearer. This was a place of great trust. The job of the cupbearer was to taste the king's drinks before him. If someone tried to poison the king, the cupbearer was the last line of defense. The cupbearer was essentially the king's secret service detail stepping in front of a bullet. Nehemiah was trusted by the king to keep him alive because not only was he willing to check the kings drink for poison, he was also the only person who had the opportunity to poison the king.

So, Nehemiah had a pretty close relationship with Artaxerxes.

If you want some more proof, one day he walked in to take him his wine and Artaxerxes said, "Hey why do you look so sad?" (Nehemiah 2:2). That reveals a close relationship. They cared about each other, but they were still work colleagues, one a Jew, one a Persian emperor. They weren't the same. Despite their differences, they had a relationship built on mutual respect and concern for each other's well-being.

So, when Artaxerxes asks "why so sad" Nehemiah, even though he was afraid, was able to make his interest known to the king. Nehemiah was a member of a conquered people. Thus, it was not an easy relationship to form. He was a servant, captured and taken from his home, but he had a relationship with his oppressor. This relationship was a choice for both parties. And that's where we can learn our first lesson: make the choice.

Nehemiah made a choice to be a desirable relationship partner. Notice that he says, "I had never been sad in his presence before" (Nehemiah 2:1). I find that to be a very telling statement. He makes a conscious, deliberate effort to present a positive emotional state to the king. He does this every day.

I can tell you with certainty that I don't do this. My job has stress, but not I-might-get-poisoned-today stress. Still, in the face of Nehemiah's job stress, in the face of being a captive, in the face of being a servant, he never showed it to the king. Amazing.

From here the story gets really interesting from an interdependence standpoint. Artaxerxes was the ruler of the Achaemenid (Persian) Empire. He was the son of Xerxes. His specific title was king of kings because his empire was so vast. His father Xerxes had been murdered by his personal bodyguard, one of the few individuals who would have access to the king of kings.

There was absolutely no reason for Artaxerxes to entertain a conversation with Nehemiah, let alone ask him what was troubling him. But he embraced interdependence. Artaxerxes was a CEO and Nehemiah's boss, to bring this story into our modern thought. Nehemiah was one of the individual contributors in a very large organization. Artaxerxes can just tell him what to do, tell him to get back to work. He can do what most organizations do today: show some concern, and then move on to the next organizational goal.

But that's not what he did. The most powerful man on Earth asked, "Tell me what's troubling you." So, Nehemiah told him Jerusalem was in ruins, the walls and gates destroyed. He was heartbroken over it.

Artaxerxes embraced the interdependence, "Tell me what you want."

This is a powerful question and I recommend you consider ways to add this into your daily negotiations. It shows concern for others and brings the power of being the provider.

This is how leaders act. It is how we separate ourselves as the best. Do we even do this at home with our kids? When we say to our child, "Unload the dishwasher" and they say, "But I have something else," (whatever that may be) do we ask what it is that's important to them? Or do we press on with the "do your chores" mantra, certain that our will is more important than theirs?

Did Artaxerxes care about the walls and gates of Jerusalem? Probably not. His father was the one who tore them down. But he did care about Nehemiah, so he asked, "What do you want?"

Nehemiah explained he wanted to rebuild the walls and gates. Artaxerxes was no fool. He could see that would benefit him as well. And leveraging the interdependence in the relationship leads to a gain for both parties. Had either party been unwilling to explore an interdependent relationship, they would have lost out on the gains. If Artaxerxes was unwilling to grant the interdependence and kept Nehemiah in a dependent relationship he would have said, "Why the long face, go fix it, I don't need to look at a sad cupbearer." If Nehemiah had been unwilling to accept the interdependent relationship, he would have replied to Artaxerxes's concern with, "Just some trouble at home, nothing for you to worry about O King of Kings."

We need to look for our opportunities to embrace the interdependence in our relationships because that's where we get the gain. Nehemiah makes a big ask. And the king knew it was a big ask because he responded, "How long do you think you will be gone?"

Artaxerxes's father was murdered by an untrustworthy servant. He didn't want to give up his most trusted servant. It was a big cost for Artaxerxes. It was also a big cost for Nehemiah. He was asking to leave a comfortable position in the palace to lead a difficult construction project. He was fearful enough about the project and its success that he made a second audacious ask. He asked the king to write letters to the governors so they would support his project.

The big question is, why? Why would either of these two powerful men enter this interdependent relationship?

The truth of interdependence is that we can achieve more by embracing an interdependent relationship than we can on our own.

The gain for Nehemiah was clear. His interest was in restoring Jerusalem. He loved his hometown and people and, due to his position of power, could benefit the Jews and rebuild the city walls.

The benefit to Artaxerxes is a little more nuanced. Jerusalem had always been an important city in the region. Having it fortified and under his control would be a benefit. But there was more here. He could benefit Nehemiah while he realized his own gain. They had a good relationship, so the king wanted to benefit his friend. Both men would benefit, the Jewish people would benefit, and the empire would benefit. This story is a great example of maximizing joint gain.

If the king sent someone other than Nehemiah, the interdependence would lose value. If Nehemiah didn't ask for the letters of safe passage, the deal would lose value. They maximized the outcome.

Interdependence within organizations represents a pivotal and transformative approach to how individuals collaborate and work together. It all begins with a fundamental notion: choice. Yes, interdependence is a choice—an intentional decision made by individuals within an organization to harness the collective power of collaboration. It is about acknowledging that, together, as a team, we can achieve far more than any one of us can alone. Interdependence is a dynamic force that reshapes traditional hierarchical structures and fosters an environment where everyone's contributions matter.

Interdependence signifies a departure from the outdated paradigm of rigid hierarchy and top-down authority. It recognizes that no single party in an organization possesses all the knowledge, skills, or resources required for success. Instead, it underscores the reality that we depend on each other. Like cogs in a well-oiled machine, we function best when we work together, complementing each other's strengths and compensating for weaknesses.

Consider the example of a team in an organization. Each team member has a unique role and set of responsibilities. In a traditional, dependent approach, team members might view themselves as separate entities working to complete tasks independently. However, the shift to interdependence transforms this outlook. Team members begin to see themselves as interconnected and interrelated components of a greater whole. They understand that their collective efforts create something more significant and more valuable than any isolated contributions.

Now, let's return to our discussion of how this concept applies to leadership within an organization. Imagine two types of bosses: one who demands obedience due to their position and another who chooses to work collaboratively with their team members to achieve the best outcomes. The difference between these two leaders is profound. The first may wield power and authority, but their approach often breeds resentment and stifles creativity. On the contrary, the second leader, who embraces interdependence, recognizes that their success is intertwined with the success of their team. They actively seek input, value diverse perspectives, and create an environment where every team member feels valued and empowered.

Interdependence plays a crucial role in organizational negotiations. Often, one party may possess more power, resources, or alternatives, which could allow them to dictate terms. However, the most successful negotiators understand the value of interdependence. They deliberately place themselves in a position where collaboration is the key to creative solutions. By doing so, they foster an environment where both parties can achieve more together than they could separately.

Interdependence brings a multitude of benefits to organizational relationships. It promotes a mindset of valuing the interests of others as much as one's own. This mindset shift is not about sacrificing individual goals but rather recognizing that aligning individual and collective interests can yield superior outcomes. It encourages the free flow of information, creating a fertile ground for innovative ideas and solutions to flourish. Moreover, interdependence builds trust—trust that stems from the willingness to share power and collaborate rather than dominate.

Interdependence is not just a concept; it's a philosophy that can revolutionize the way organizations function. It's about making a conscious choice to work together, recognizing that we are all connected and that our collective efforts can lead to better relationships, increased trust, and superior outcomes for everyone involved. Embrace interdependence, implement it in your organizational interactions, and watch as it transforms the way your team and your entire organization operate.

chapter 13

Negotiation is an integral part of our personal and professional lives. How we approach negotiations and treat the other parties involved are crucial factors that influence the outcomes. In this chapter, we will delve deep into the *art* of negotiation, emphasizing the significance of empathy, perspective-taking, and collaboration to ensure our interactions are grounded first in treating others with dignity and respect.

Some scholars have advocated for removing emotion from your negotiation interactions. While it may sound nice, it doesn't do justice to the interaction or the people with whom we are negotiating. Emotional content is important to the negotiation and to decision-making. Daniel Kahneman spent his career studying the nonrational aspects of decision-making. Kahneman found that while many of our decisions consider rational or economic outcomes, they include so much more that is not rational. Jonathan Haidt, in his book, *The Happiness Hypothesis*, demonstrates the importance of speaking to both the rational and emotional decision-making aspects in an interaction. Haidt tells us that the rational aspects can control the emotional aspects to an extent, but neither is complete without the other.

People make decisions using more information than just rational economic data. The best negotiators appeal to both aspects of decisions. The rational mind demands that we present positions that are reasonable. The rational mind is very aware

PUTTING INTERESTS FIRST

of the offers, concessions, and final outcomes. The emotional mind is tuned in to interests. The emotional mind is looking for fulfillment of the "why" in the negotiation. We need to address the emotional aspects to best fulfill the interests in the negotiation. This includes understanding the emotional aspects of decision-making in the other parties involved. We need to be aware of how we interact, how we address the emotions, and how we see the problem from their perspective.

People are concerned about the fairness of their outcome and the fairness of the process to reach the outcome, but the biggest concern is usually interpersonal fairness or how we interact. That means, if we treat people with dignity and respect, that form of fairness is more important to them than the outcome or process.

In modern negotiations, achieving success is not just about personal gain; it's about finding mutual value, fostering positive relationships, and leveraging interdependence to benefit everyone involved. Whether you're negotiating large deals in the business world or navigating everyday interactions, the principles outlined here will help you enhance your negotiation skills.

The letter to the Thessalonians addresses the idea of consideration and respect due others.

> *"Now we ask you, brothers and sisters, to acknowledge those who work hard among you, who care for you in the Lord and who admonish you. Hold them in the highest regard in love because of their work. Live in peace with each other. And we urge you, brothers and sisters, warn those who are idle and disruptive, encourage the disheartened, help the weak, be patient with everyone. Make sure that nobody pays back wrong for wrong, but always strive to do what is good for each other and for everyone else"* (1 Thessalonians 5:12-15).

Treating others with dignity and respect is the first step to speaking to both the rational and the emotional aspects of a negotiation. Once that threshold is reached, empathy and perspective-taking form the bedrock of effective negotiations. Research has consistently shown that these qualities are paramount in building trust, finding creative solutions, and ultimately achieving better outcomes. It's essential to understand the role empathy and perspective-taking play and how they are connected to dignity and respect.

Empathy involves the ability to understand and share the feelings of others. Without empathy, we can't address the emotions of the others involved in the negotiation. Empathy allows us to connect on a deeper level with our negotiation partners. When we genuinely empathize with their emotions and concerns, the foundation for a more productive and respectful interaction is laid. This doesn't mean that if they are angry or sad we must present as angry or sad. What this means is that when others in the negotiation are presenting emotional content, we should acknowledge and value it. *"Oh, it seems that something is bothering you today? Is it something that you want to discuss? Or would like to postpone our interaction until a better time?"* This values the others in the negotiation and allows for the emotional content while not letting the emotions be the most important part of the interaction.

Perspective-taking, on the other hand, is the art of stepping into the shoes of the other party. It requires us to consider their viewpoint, needs, and desires. By doing so, we gain valuable insights into their motivations and can work together to find mutually beneficial solutions. If we only understand the interaction from our own perspective, we miss opportunity and creative solutions.

It was noted earlier that Roger Fisher, known for his groundbreaking work in negotiation, emphasized the significance of perspective-taking. In his influential book, *Getting to Yes* (first published in 1988 and rereleased in 1992), Fisher revolutionized negotiation practices. He advocated for a shift away from adversarial, secretive tactics and towards collaborative, value-driven negotiations.

Fisher's legacy continues to shape modern negotiation principles. He believed that a negotiator's most important skill is the ability to take the perspective of the other party. By doing so, negotiators can transcend traditional win-lose scenarios and strive for mutually beneficial agreements.

In any negotiation, having clear and well-defined goals is essential. Your success depends on your ability to articulate your objectives effectively. Whether you're negotiating in a business context or making personal decisions, knowing what you want to achieve is paramount.

What we don't think about is, why? And the answer often surprises students; it may surprise you also. You aren't negotiating for the outcome, you are negotiating for what the outcome achieves for you. But if you don't know this, you could spend a lot of time fighting about a price, or a delivery date, or a discount, when that's not the most important aspect of the negotiation.

You must know why you are negotiating and use that to drive all your interactions. We call this goal the interest in the negotiation. Your negotiations are never about money, but we often focus on money because it's tangible, measurable, and easily understood. The measurable aspects of your negotiation are the actualization of the interest, the why.

Focusing on interests demonstrates that you are not just seeking personal gain but are genuinely interested in obtaining value for yourself and providing value to the other party. It sets the stage for a collaborative negotiation where both sides can work together to achieve their respective goals.

In most negotiations there are multiple parties with diverse interests, and their goals are interdependent. Successful negotiation hinges on understanding and addressing the concerns of all parties involved. This level of empathy and perspective-taking is essential for achieving mutually beneficial outcomes. If the focus is on positions, the negotiation becomes more difficult for all. If the focus is on interests—why each party desires the outcome—it can fundamentally change the interaction. Effective negotiation is not about giving up on your goals; it's about balancing your goals with those of the other parties involved. While it's natural to focus on your desired outcomes, it's equally important to understand and address the goals of your negotiation partners.

Emphasizing the importance of perspective-taking means approaching negotiations with a mindset of collaboration and compassion. Instead of merely advocating for your position, focus on understanding and facilitating the goals of all involved parties. One important part of that facilitation is the ability to facilitate meaningful discussions. It's not just about getting what you want; it's about ensuring that all parties benefit from the interaction. This facilitation role involves asking questions, seeking deeper understanding, and building trust. Questions should focus on the interests in the interaction. You should ask a lot of "why" questions in the negotiation to help lead to information about interests. Too often negotiators focus on the "how much" questions and then find themselves in an adversarial situation.

It's important to note that facilitating discussions and seeking understanding does not mean giving up on your goals. Rather, it's about finding common ground and identifying opportunities for mutual gain.

Some older negotiation strategies promote tactics like dominating the conversation, creating negative emotional states in your negotiation partner, or even allowing them to maintain incorrect information. However, these outdated approaches can lead to unproductive and hostile negotiations.

Research consistently shows that fostering positive emotional states, providing accurate information, and building trust yield better results. Instead of seeking to gain an advantage through manipulation, we should aim to elevate the negotiation process through collaboration and empathy.

In negotiations, we must aim for mutual benefit. The philosophy of munificence, believing that there is an abundance of resources and opportunities, should guide our approach. Negotiation is not a zero-sum game where one party's gain is another's loss; it's a chance to create value for everyone involved.

Also, it's important to share information about your interests. Rather than keeping information secret or exploiting others' lack of understanding, we should be transparent and empower our negotiation partners with accurate information. By fostering a collaborative environment, we can all achieve more significant and sustainable outcomes.

This is supported by what Paul writes to Timothy.

> *"Command those who are rich in this present world not to be arrogant nor to put their hope in wealth, which is so uncertain, but to put their hope in God, who richly provides us with everything for our enjoyment. Command them to do good, to be rich in good deeds, and to be generous and willing to share. In this way they will lay up treasure for themselves as a firm foundation for the coming age, so that they may take hold of the life that is truly life"* (1 Timothy 6:17-19).

Our goal should be to move away from outdated negotiation strategies that focus on manipulation and domination. Instead, aim for mutual benefit, viewing negotiation as an opportunity to create value and build positive relationships. By approaching negotiations with compassion and collaboration, you can achieve your goals while also helping others achieve theirs, ultimately leading to more successful and fulfilling interactions.

Can you make better offers? Are some offers better than others? Let's examine three key aspects of making an offer. We'll explore how to leverage these aspects to enhance your negotiation strategies and discuss their impact on the negotiation process and outcomes. This will provide a detailed analysis of the importance of offers, specifically focusing on the timing, content, and focus of your proposals.

Let's begin with the timing of your offer. When should you introduce your offer? There are two critical components to consider: how early in the negotiation process and whether you want to be the first to make an offer.

It's essential to be aware of the dynamics in the negotiation when considering when to make an offer. First, take some time to build trust. Do this by building the relationships, by being consistent in your behavior, and by using interdependence in a manner that maximizes the available resources to be shared in the interaction. This is a deliberate process that is often pursued recklessly. Throwing an offer too early, before all parties are ready, can alienate, raise suspicion, and negatively impact trust. Building these essential relationships takes time, and it involves discussing motives and identifying shared interdependence. You need to have discussions about interests to get a deeper understanding of the reasons each party has entered the negotiation. This requires careful planning and

chapter 14

CREATIVE SOLUTIONS

commitment, including preparing scripted questions and thoughts on how to articulate your interests.

Should you be the first to make an offer?

Research indicates a strong correlation between first offers and final outcomes. Being the first to propose an offer anchors the negotiation, setting the tone for subsequent discussions. To control the narrative effectively, your initial offer must be well-reasoned, connecting your interests and the shared interdependence with others. This means you should be well-prepared, knowing your motives and objectives before entering the negotiation. The notion that "whoever speaks first loses" arises when individuals are unprepared to make a meaningful first offer. If you are prepared, you should make the first offer. If you defer the first offer to the other party, you give them control over the negotiation.

The content of your offers conveys valuable information to all parties involved. Regardless of your level of preparation, your offers communicate your values. Avoid making random or ungrounded offers, as these can mislead and hinder your progress. Instead, ensure that each offer aligns with your interests and motives. If your interests differ significantly from others, your offers should reflect this, making it clear that a deal may be challenging to achieve. Open dialogue about these differences can help build trust and understanding, ultimately benefiting the negotiation. Often, people think they should hide issues in their offers or make their offers difficult. Don't forget that offers are just suggested positions that represent the achievement of your interests. There are other ways to achieve your interests; your offer is just one way.

In class, I ask my students, who are about to enter the job market, what it would take for a company to hire you if they didn't pay money. It's a ridiculous thought experiment to some, but if you really think it through, you can learn a lot about what you are trying to achieve with your employment. Is it just the standard of living? Or do you want some freedom from your job? Do you want an intellectual challenge? Do you want to be respected in your community?

Finally, consider the focus of your offers, which may be the most crucial aspect. Your offers should consistently direct attention to the primary motive behind the negotiation. While tangible positions, such as price or delivery dates, are essential, they should not overshadow the underlying interests. Emphasize the reason for negotiating, as it opens various possibilities to meet your interests. Don't fall into the trap of fixating solely on positions, as this limits your options for success.

Here are some tactical guidelines for making effective offers.

Be prepared to move first when the opportunity arises. This means that most of the work in a negotiation happens before the interaction. You have to walk in ready to make that first offer, and if others involved in the negotiation beat you to it, you will already be prepared with a counteroffer.

Present offers decisively, avoiding hesitation or uncertainty. If you sound hesitant, it negatively impacts trust. It will increase suspicion that you are hiding something. It also invites contentious behavior. If you make a hesitant offer, the others involved may be more willing to oppose you, may be less willing to give concessions, and may hold to their positions very tightly.

Keep your offers static with clear reasons and justifications. If you give a range, you are introducing ambiguity into the interaction. Think about how a range is perceived if the hiring manager asks you what you would like for your salary. If you say, *"Well, somewhere in the range of 80 to 100 thousand."* You are focused on the top number ($100,000), but the hiring manager only heard that you would be willing to take as low as $80,000. Also, be sure to give a well-thought-out and deliberate reason when you present an offer. Substantiate your ask with a solid reason.

Don't be worried if your offer is accepted without extensive haggling; it can be a sign of a well-thought-out proposal. I often get asked, "What do you do if they accept your first offer?" I shake their hand, say thank you, and ask them if this was a great deal for them, too. You should be prepared with a great first offer that gets all your interests met. If the others involved agree, great. Move on and know that the next time you negotiate with them, it will be even easier to get a great outcome.

Listen to the other party's offers and try to understand their perspective. Don't make the mistake of using the time that others are presenting their interests, positions, and information to prepare what you are going to say. Have your thoughts together, prepare so that you can look at bullet points and say what you want to say. Respect others while they speak; it will go a long way to a better outcome.

Be open to discussing both your interests and theirs, seeking hidden value. Don't hide your interests. You may think that you are reserving power for yourself, but you aren't. You are giving away the opportunity to get more by uncovering ways that the other parties can satisfy those interests.

Expect that concessions will be requested and be willing to engage in further negotiation. Concessions are an important part of negotiation. Concessions move the parties toward interest achievement. But, be prepared to make concessions. Don't give them on the fly. Know before you start the interaction which issues you can and will concede. Know which issues are important to you and which are not. If an issue isn't important to you and doesn't have much value, the worst thing you can do is to say, "I don't really care about that issue." Instead, you should say, "I have some flexibility on that issue if you can benefit me on this other issue that's important to me." Use the issues in the negotiation to move everyone toward the best outcome possible.

Always consider the other party's perspective when making an offer. Avoid blocking out their point of view. This will not only make you a better negotiator but also a better person.

Offers are potent tools that shape the course of a negotiation. By mastering the timing, content, and focus of your offers, you can enhance your negotiation skills, foster trust, and work towards more favorable outcomes. Deliberate, well-researched offers are key to successful negotiations.

All of this is meaningless without trust. In fact, every relationship you have, every interaction you have, comes down to trust. Without trust, we cannot maximize the benefits that we get from the interaction. We cannot maximize the process. Everything becomes a question.

Think about how your world would look without trust. Certainly, your closest relationships would fall apart. If you're married or have a significant other, imagine that relationship without trust. Neither of you would be able to leave the house. Your friendships would fail, and your peer groups at church and at work would not function the way we have all agreed as a society to do things.

Without trust, you wouldn't be able to work. Your employer couldn't count on you to get the job done, and you couldn't count on being paid. I get paid once a month in my job. I trust that after doing a month's worth of work, my employer will pay me the agreed-upon wage. My employer trusts that I, and the thousands of other employees, will do the jobs as we agreed for that month. It only works with trust. If we have no trust, the employer would have to be present as I work and hand me payment continuously as the service is rendered or product produced. And that would be the end of our economy.

chapter 15

Think about how we get paid today. I never see a paycheck. My bank account just increases appropriately on payday. That's trust. But even if I did see a paycheck, it's still an exercise in trust. The employer hands me a piece of paper that essentially says, "Trust that I'm good for the money." If you are paid in cash, you are trusting the issuer of the currency and the greater currency market in the world.

Cash is king, my friend and colleague John Schoen always said, but a look at history will tell us that the first paper money printed in North America was printed by the Confederate States of America. And it was a promise. It asked for trust. The Confederate dollar was a promissory note that stated, "Six months after the ratification of a treaty of peace between the Confederate States and the United States," the bill would be exchanged for the appropriate amount of silver or gold by the Confederate government. The money was a question of trust. By the end of 1864, as the Civil War was nearing its end and the United States was the obvious victor, one Confederate dollar was worth three cents in US currency. The trust was lost.

There are several antecedents to define trust. I will explain those that are most important to our interactions and to our negotiations but don't think that I am going to give you the secret to trust. Trust is a complex construct, one that has been studied extensively but is still not completely understood. The good news is that we have a significant knowledge of trust, such that we can at least understand and have some control over it. I'll break it down for you in this chapter. Trust me.

What is trust? The construct of trust is built from ideas that were explored in Sociology, Social Psychology, and Organizational Behavior. These areas of study, while diverse, are all constant in the fact that they are concerned with the interaction of people. However, as ubiquitous as the idea of trust is in organizational life, its meaning and understanding have been relatively loose. In fact, in 1975, well-known scholar Lyman Porter and his colleagues called the concept of organizational trust vague. If the top minds in the field didn't have a clear understanding of the concept, how could we?

Since that time, we have made strides in understanding trust, but it's still a mystery in some respects. The modern definition of trust is, "the extent to which a person is confident in, and willing to act on the basis of, the words, action, and decisions of another" (McAllister, 1995). In terms of what we can all embrace, trust is the feeling that you can count on someone to do what they say they will do. We usually don't make attempts to measure trust in our everyday interactions, but we are aware of our levels of trust with various people. It's that innate awareness that makes trust difficult to understand. You know it when you have it. You also know when it's absent.

Research has differentiated between various flavors of trust. The first differentiation is the level at which the trust is aimed. If we are talking about trust in a person, we call it interpersonal trust. If we are talking about trust in an organization, we call it organizational trust. If we are talking about trust in systems, we call it impersonal trust.

So, interpersonal trust would speak to the trust that you have in specific people, whether within your organization or outside of it. This could mean trust in your boss, specific coworkers, or individuals in your family. This trust is built person-to-person. There are a lot of instances in which interpersonal is the kind of trust we are applying. This is the type of trust that usually activates when involved in a negotiation. While a lot of our business negotiations happen within organizations, most of the time, we negotiate with another person.

Organizational trust is what allows us to be confident in our interactions with an organization. Oftentimes, when we are involved with businesses, we build some interpersonal trust. I know when I was in sales, many of the relationships that I built were ongoing with the same individuals at these organizations. I would build a relationship with the purchasing agent in the organization, and she would be my main contact. However, if I wasn't available to help her, the trust that I had built would be imbued to the others within the organization, and they would be trusted by her in my absence.

Impersonal trust is trust in systems. So, if you do the things necessary to reach the promotion plateau and you believe that the greater HR complex in your organization will reward you for it, you are trusting in the system.

How do we build trust? Trust is built on a complex framework. In every relationship, in every interaction, trust must be built, and it is somewhat idiosyncratic. Now, as I have done throughout the book, I want to bring in the spiritual aspect. Trust is something inherent in the Christian experience. The concept should be relatively familiar to anyone who has a level of understanding of the Bible. In fact, the Bible and Christian life are built on faith and trust. The Christian lives a life of faith trusting that the promises of God are real. The Christian faith is built on a belief that 2,000 years ago, God's Son walked the earth, died, and rose as our Savior.

As the writer to the Hebrews puts it in the eleventh chapter, *"Faith is the confidence that what we hope for will actually happen."* This is trust. Think back to the example about your paycheck. Trust is the confidence that your organization will pay you for the work you've done, which is what we are all hoping. So, trust is a Biblical concept. Faith and trust are very similar concepts. Faith is the religious expression of trust. And it is a religious expression, not a Christian expression. If you believe in something other than the Bible as your truth, you still have faith; it's just placed elsewhere. If you believe there is no deity, you are placing your faith in the fact that there is no deity.

The same can be said for trust. If my organization is trustworthy, then I have a hope that once a month my bank account will increase. Trust demands faithfulness. What can we do to demonstrate faithfulness? What is it that builds trust?

Several antecedents of trust are important to consider in order to impact our interactions. We evaluate whether we should trust someone based on the legitimacy and transparency of their communication.

Legitimacy is an antecedent of trust that speaks to the desirableness or appropriateness of one's actions. This all happens within the system of norms and beliefs in which that person or organization operates. Legitimacy speaks to whether the actions or words are believable and within the boundary conditions and norms of the situation.

Interpersonal trust is built from person to person. It is built in relationship and interaction. We can't have interpersonal trust without some experience with the individual in question.

There are ways to move forward without trust. We can use a tit-for-tat strategy. Though unsustainable, this has been shown to be a productive way to move forward.

Currently, my concern revolves around my air conditioning system. Despite the end of summer, Texas remains scorching, with temperatures hovering around 98 degrees. My air conditioner isn't working right, and as I sit here in my home office, sweating like crazy, I'm thinking about who I should trust for repairs.

This is an important trust. I know exactly who to contact if my AC breaks. I have a long relationship with a person with whom I used to attend church. So, I called him and got his voicemail, because everyone is having trouble with their AC after this long hot summer. I left a message, hopeful. Within ten minutes I got a call back from him. "Hey, Chris, I can come over tomorrow morning," he said, even though the next day was Saturday.

This trust is a significant factor in my decision-making process. My first encounter with this person was when my son was a baby (eighteen years ago) and my AC went out, on a weekend, of course. My wife and I saw him and his wife at church. Of course, they wanted to see the baby and asked how it was going. We said, "It's hot at our house. The AC is down." He said, "OK, we'll, see you after church and I'll get it fixed for you." He did. I recommend him to everyone I can. Because I trust him. People who trust me, trust him by proxy.

Trust often evolves through continued interactions and consistent experiences with individuals. It necessitates working with the same people over an extended period. This can be both positive and negative as we develop trust in knowing how others will react or respond over time. This is the most common way that we develop trust. Until we have had significant enough interactions with an individual, we don't usually build trust.

There are three important factors when we build trust. The first is consistency. Consistency is very important to the trust-building process. This is where we check if actions, words, and reputation are in line with expectations. As you may guess, consistency takes time. Actions need to be observed over time and then checked against a standard. After enough time, we can develop trust because there is significant consistency between words, actions, and reputations. This amount of time can vary based on the prior relationship, whether there is any reason given to question the trust, and the overall consistency of the interactions.

It's not always possible to take the time to build trust based on consistency. There are times and contexts in which trust needs to happen more quickly. Fortunately, we have a lot of reputation information available to use to make our trust decisions. Trust that forms based on those recommendations and reviews is called quick trust. This quick trust allows us to decide about whether a person, organization, or service deserves our trust based on the trust that has developed with others.

In today's connected world, there is a lot of source material that can help us decide to trust. It's essential to be discerning in our use of recommendations and reviews. We should rely on quality recommendations from credible sources and consider both positive and negative reviews to gain a balanced perspective.

The final possibility to allow negotiated outcomes is to use proxies for trust. Contracts and contingencies act as proxies for trust, as they provide a structured framework for negotiations. They reduce the need for trust by specifying agreed-upon consequences for certain actions. In the place of a long-term relationship that builds trust over time, we can use a legal document that specifies a penalty for breaking trust. If a legal document isn't the right tool, we can build contingencies into the negotiated agreement that specify different outcomes for actions that meet or do not meet the agreed upon expectations. It's important to ensure that these tools encourage cooperation and success rather than focusing solely on punitive measures. Clear and fair contingencies should be established.

When aiming to build trust over time, several key principles are important.

Consistency is paramount. Actions and words must align consistently with prior behavior and commitments. Inconsistencies erode trust.

Transparency is essential in good communication. Openness about what can and cannot be shared fosters trust. You don't have to share everything you know, but you should never lie or try to hide information. It's much better to let someone know that they are asking about information that you prefer to keep private.

Finally, choosing consistent and transparent partners is crucial when aiming to build trust over time. Interactions with untrustworthy individuals can hinder trust development. Adhering to the agreed-upon conditions and avoiding seeking loopholes or exploiting contingencies is essential, as doing so risks damaging trust.

Understanding the origins of trust, the methods for building it, and the principles for maintaining it are vital components of successful negotiations and interactions. Trust is a powerful element in human relationships, and by applying these principles, we can navigate these interactions more effectively.

Now that you know more about negotiation, you have what I call the burden of being well-informed. Don't worry, this burden isn't too heavy—not as heavy as the burden of blissful ignorance. What this means is that when you enter any negotiation situation, when you have an interaction that has some level of interdependence, the burden is on you to teach. The burden is on you to guide. The burden is on you to work with the other parties involved toward a joint gain. You can't just drop back to a competitive style because everyone else is doing it. You know what that costs now. You know the stories, the research, and the Christian principles that demand a joint gain approach.

We don't all have the same background, and we shouldn't expect everyone to have the same knowledge. For example, my uncle had a great deal of knowledge about fly fishing and cigar smoking. He had the burden of being well-informed in those two areas, and he took that burden very seriously. There were many mornings in my early teens that I rose long before the sun and rode in my uncle's old truck to the river where he unburdened himself by tirelessly teaching me the skills to cast a fly while smoking a cigar. He didn't have some of the other knowledge necessary in life, particularly most of the skills that I've written about in this book. If he hadn't died at a young age, I would feel compelled to help him with these skills.

That's the point of the joint gain view of

chapter 16

NO SCOREBOARD

negotiation. It's not a method to dominate others. It's not a method to ensure we get our outcome. It's not something that should be hidden so that others can't use it against us like so many other negotiation or persuasion ideas. Joint gain is more powerful when we share the idea. When we go into the interaction and start by telling the other party that we really do want them to get a great outcome, but we are honest enough to tell them we also want a great outcome. And together we can get to that outcome, but we have to work together and leverage the strength that we have together.

This method takes more time. This method isn't easy. It demands a commitment to the joint gain idea, and it demands that we spread the word about it.

Happiness Is Not the Measure

Be open to thinking critically about how you measure success in your negotiations and be willing to adjust and accept that maybe new information is going to give you a different perspective. Your goal in negotiation is not to be happy at the end of the interaction. I'm not saying this to be controversial or contrarian. The statement isn't clickbait. I want you to really think about your goal.

Everything should point back to your interest in the negotiation. The interest should drive your behavior and be the motivation, that reason for the interaction. Absolutely everything should point back to that interest. If we start our preparation with the interest as the guide, we should use that as the measure when we are done to see if we achieved the reason for the negotiation.

Many times, when we get to the end, we look at our outcome and use comparison as the measure of whether we've met our interest.

Certainly, there are negotiations, primarily in the personal realm, where happiness is the outcome that we're trying to achieve. Think about how family negotiations fall into this category. When I get in the car with my wife and we do the negotiation that many married couples do, we talk about where we're going to go for dinner, happiness is the outcome we're after. So, there are times when happiness is an appropriate measure.

But when we're talking about organizational goals, a happiness focus doesn't align with what we're trying to achieve. Let me give you a couple of reasons why happiness doesn't work well as a measure of our success in our organizational negotiations.

The first is that happiness is somewhat disconnected from our interests. A lot of times we rely on whether we've achieved our positional bargaining goals that we set rather than pointing directly back to our interests as a measure of success in our negotiations. If we go into a negotiation for a new car, we have some interests underlying the positions—we want a safe car for the family, we want reliable transportation, etc. We have to give and take on those positions in order to achieve the interest. If we have an emotional connection to the car, we will drive off in our dream car. That impacts how we view the interaction.

Another reason to be cautious about using happiness as a primary measure in negotiation is the psychological process called "sensemaking." Karl Weick studied this concept extensively. Sensemaking involves revisiting past events and crafting a narrative to explain them, typically with a positive bias. Emotions, such as happiness, play a role in this process. Initially, we experience emotional reactions, primarily in the amygdala, and subsequently engage in sensemaking to understand these emotions. This suggests that happiness is somewhat flexible. We can frame a negative outcome as happiness by engaging in sensemaking, constructing a reality that aligns with our desired emotional response. Consequently, happiness becomes an unreliable measure influenced by our sensemaking tendencies.

Revisiting the car purchase scenario, we can justify the interaction, both the process and the outcome. It may not be the outcome that we thought we would get—we may have paid too much, or, God forbid, bought the wheel protection program—but we make it a good deal in our mind. We make it make sense. That leads to happiness.

The problem with sensemaking is it is somewhat disconnected from the interest. The interest may have been to get reliable transportation for the family at a specific price with some specific conditions, and yet, somehow, we drove off the lot in a 1978 Corvette Stingray. We go through a sensemaking process to justify the outcome. *"This is a 25th Anniversary Edition Stingray. A priceless classic car."* But you can't fit any groceries in it. Or any kids. And it's old, and maybe not very reliable. Your interest was not met. You might be happy, but you failed in your negotiation. This is an extreme example, but you can imagine less extreme examples, probably some that happened this week.

The third challenge with happiness as a measure for negotiation outcomes is its reliance on our internal evaluation. Often, we neglect to invest the time, effort, and thought required for a meaningful assessment of happiness; instead, we rely on gut feelings. We ask ourselves, "Does this feel good?"

However, the fact that some things may feel good in the moment does not mean they are genuinely beneficial. It's usually upon later reflection that we recognize this. The transient emotion of happiness complicates matters; once it fades, is it still a favorable outcome?

The issue becomes particularly crucial in organizational contexts where complex interactions and external pressures abound. Organizations often set specific metrics and goals, adding complexity to the sensemaking process. In this environment, we have ample opportunities to shape explanations for our outcomes, focusing on the positive aspects to foster a sense of happiness.

Rather than resorting to rhetoric that frames outcomes as wins or losses, we should recognize that negotiation serves a different purpose. Negotiation is about leveraging interdependence to achieve more collectively than we could individually. These interactions are intricate and often ongoing, fostering relationships and recurring negotiations.

Instead of seeking a simplistic scorecard, we should consider using our interests as the ultimate metric for success. Our interests represent why we are negotiating in the first place, and meeting these interests should be the true measure of a successful outcome. It doesn't matter if the outcome is larger or smaller than that of the other party; what matters is whether our interests were met and whether we successfully created value through interdependence.

We need to shift our focus away from traditional scorekeeping and winning or losing mentalities in negotiations. Instead, we should prioritize understanding and meeting our interests as the ultimate measure of success. This approach aligns with the complex and multiparty nature of negotiations, allowing us to create value and build strong relationships over time.

It is possible to have a successful life and a successful career and ignore all the principles in this book. You can live a life completely focused on your own outcomes. But is that what you want? Can you leave a trail of selfish destruction while truly gaining for yourself?

There's a better way to live. Benefiting others and benefiting yourself are not different ends of the spectrum. You can do both. And in so doing leave a legacy of kindness and success for everyone.

I'm currently training a puppy. It doesn't always make sense trying to get a dog to do the things that you want it to do. I'm training my puppy to do scent work, to find things based on smell. It's a skill that is used in airports, sports venues, helping in search and rescue operations, and competing in trials to find things that they don't naturally care about. I was at a seminar to help me train my dog. The presenter said, "We can't really control the dog, but we can build a tendency in them." He has a lot of experience. He was one of the individuals, along with his dog, who was tasked with finding survivors and bodies on September 11 at the World Trade Center. He had a dog that went into burning rubble to find humans. Dogs don't like to go into dangerous situations like this, and they don't naturally find humans.

This is how I want you to think about negotiation. It's not a natural situation. There are no "born negotiators." This is something we must learn deliberately. Once we learn it and do it over and over in the best way, we build a tendency. That's a powerful idea. This book is meant to give you guidance in your negotiations so that you can build a tendency in your interactions. A tendency is a powerful default condition for our

CONCLUSION

interactions. If we implement a joint gain tendency, it can greatly improve our outcomes.

What that looks like for negotiation is:

First, we need to abandon the win mentality in exchange for joint gains. We need to step away from win-win thinking and language when it comes to negotiation, and we must stop talking about beating others. We must stop comparing outcomes to others' outcomes and start comparing outcomes to interests. There can't be competitive negotiation with the joint gain mindset. The motive in our negotiations must be collaborative—a motive that builds up outcomes for all negotiators involved.

Coupled with that, we need to adopt a munificence mentality. Remember, munificence is the idea that resources are abundant. We can't have an outlook based on scarcity. The scarcity mindset expects a competitive negotiation. It's not the tendency that we are trying to build. We are trying to build the tendency to expect more, to bring more to the table, to provide more value.

Once we have our motive straight, we need to focus on the deliberate nature of our interactions. Engage in the motive to provide value. Bring value to the table, share information, and benefit others—all while ensuring that we are achieving our interest. We must be willing to question our own positions. This is how we can get to more creative outcomes. We need to remember to hold on to our interest tightly but hold our positions loosely.

We need to be sure that we are using these deliberate actions to benefit all those involved in the negotiation. That means benefiting ourselves as well. We must seek to be the most desirable negotiation partner, the person with whom everyone wants to negotiate because we provide value. Because we are honest, we share information appropriately, we have boundaries, and we are clear about those boundaries. Because we treat people with dignity and respect.

You can be the most desirable partner because that leads to more opportunities, which means increased outcomes.

You can be the most desirable partner because it's in line with your beliefs, your ethics, and your integrity.

After you've made the deal, don't be afraid to ask if it can get better. Be open to making it better, even if it gets better only for the others involved. Care about the others involved in the negotiation. Build the relationships, build your reputation as a negotiator that can be trusted.

Build a tendency for negotiation that makes you proud. Build a tendency that shows the world that you believe there is a just God and that you are His representative.

My dog is named Fearless because she is. I've never had a dog that was so smart, so strong-willed, and so determined to achieve. I named her before I knew she would represent her name so well. I think part of the naming came from my own desire to live a life without fear. Fear is why we don't trust others. Fear is why we don't benefit others but instead focus on our own gains. Fear is why we don't get more from our interactions. I want to live a life without that fear.

I encourage you, too, to live a life without fear. Build that tendency. Negotiate without fear. Fear of loss, fear of scarcity, fear of looking foolish, fear of others taking advantage of you. Build a tendency against that fear.

If you negotiate with integrity and remember that you are tasked with saying no to bad deals, you can negotiate without fear. If you are willing to build the tendency to be different in negotiation and maintain that difference in the face of the typical competitive negotiator, you can be better.

This view is supported by science. This view is supported Biblically. And if you search deep inside who you are, I bet this is the negotiator who you want to be—the negotiator who is willing to be different and better; the negotiator who is not willing to compromise and settle for less. You can be the negotiator who settles for more.

This book was a long time in the making. It started as a question from a small group of executives in Dallas. After that, a chance meeting with a former mobster led me to a literary agent who believed in what I had to say. It sounds random but was obviously guided by God's hand. I thank God for giving me the curiosity to pursue this question and the gifts to produce this book.

This project would not have been possible without the support of my family. They allowed me to go off-script and do something that at times seemed to me to be an ego project. Thank you to Stacey for always refocusing me on the good that could come from sharing this. Thank you to my children—Elyse and Jack, Harris, and Griffin—for listening to all my ideas, good and bad. This book happened because of my family, and for my family. I hope that it does the good in the world that they all saw in it from the start.

Thank you to my parents, John and Kay, my in-laws, John, and Lonna and Bob, for believing in what I was doing, even when they weren't sure what it was.

Thank you to the spiritual leaders—Ryan, Brandon, Steve, and others—who kept my eyes on the reason for the book and (hopefully) kept me away from heresy. Thank you to Aaron for the discussions and support around music, writing, and creativity. You all helped me to find where I belong.

I wouldn't have been able to write this without my academic training. Thank you to Don, John, Ingrid, and Remus for your guidance. Thank you to Stephen, Federico, Kelly, Cindy, and Dustin for all the help you gave me through grad school and

ACKNOWLEDGEMENTS

beyond. Thank you to those who came after and befriended and supported me - Pedro, Ted, Jeff, Joe, Ray, John, and Fred. I thank those who were there when I was in the early stages of talking this idea into being—the 254 crew, Mark, Gary, and Brian.

I would also like to thank the team at the Fedd Agency and Fedd Books. Thank you, Esther, for believing that I had something to say. Thank you to Brittney for keeping me focused despite all my attempts to procrastinate. Danielle and the marketing team were great. And thank you to my editors—Jason, Abner, and Kevin, for making this manuscript into something better and more readable. Any mistakes or misstatements in this book belong to me despite their best efforts.

I am thankful for all the students who asked questions, pushed boundaries, and refined my thinking. Your involvement in the process was invaluable. I would not have been able to express these ideas and teach them through this book, without first teaching them to you and learning from your feedback. Those of you that are featured in the book as examples hold a special place in my history. Your implementation of my ideas made a mark on me, so much so that your stories have become an unforgettable part of the narrative.

The process of writing this book and reflecting on the content has improved my life. My hope for this book is that it improves the life of the reader. At the very least, I want you to think about your interactions with others. We can all improve our lives. The way to do that is through Jesus. Accepting Jesus, embracing a God-pleasing life, will make everything better. I'm not endorsing prosperity gospel and saying that if you do the things in this book, you will get rich, get promotions, or get everything you've dreamed. I am saying if you embrace Jesus and do things his way, as I do my best to outline in the book, your life will be better. Better because you'll be closer to God, who loves you.